MW00990199

De Gustibus

De Gustibus

Arguing about Taste and Why We Do It

Peter Kivy

OXFORD
UNIVERSITY PRESS

OXFORD

UNIVERSITY PRESS

Great Clarendon Street, Oxford, OX2 6DP,
United Kingdom

Oxford University Press is a department of the University of Oxford.
It furthers the University's objective of excellence in research, scholarship,
and education by publishing worldwide. Oxford is a registered trade mark of
Oxford University Press in the UK and in certain other countries

First Edition published in 2015
Impression: 1

Published in the United States of America by Oxford University Press
198 Madison Avenue, New York, NY 10016, United States of America

British Library Cataloguing in Publication Data
Data available

Library of Congress Control Number: 2015938776

ISBN 978-0-19-874678-2

Printed and bound by
CPI Group (UK) Ltd, Croydon, CR0 4YY

For Ted Cohen
Never To Be Forgotten

Contents

Preface

The seed from which this monograph sprouted was planted some thirty odd years ago—1980, to be precise—in an essay of mine called "A Failure of Aesthetic Emotivism," *Philosophical Studies*, 38 (1980), pp. 351–65, portions of which, now in revised form, are included here in Chapter 4 and Chapter 5 with kind permission of Springer Science+Business Media.

I do not at present really recall how the idea for this article came to me. For at the time, the so-called emotive theory of ethics was dead as the Dodo bird, and *why* I should have been thinking about it at all I cannot imagine. Be that as it may, the point I made in that essay was that contrary to what might, on first reflection, be thought, the emotive theory of ethics was *more* plausible in at least one respect than was the emotive theory of aesthetics, namely, it provided a plausible explanation for why we engage in *ethical* disputes, whereas the latter provided none for why we engage in aesthetic disputes, disputes over taste, which manifestly we *do*.

Furthermore, I was even emboldened, in that essay, to suggest that, again contrary to what one might initially conjecture, aesthetic realism might, in the event, be a more defensible position than ethical realism. But there I essentially let the matter drop; and although in 1992 I went over much of the same ground again in an invited essay for the *Library of Living Philosophers* volume devoted to A. J. Ayer, I got no further with it, and the whole thing quietly slipped my mind.

But whereas I do not now recall why I became concerned with the emotive theory of value in the first place, in 1980, I know quite well what reminded me of it not very long ago, and what led me to the writing of the present monograph. I was invited, in 2012, to comment on a paper of James Harold's, at the Pacific Division meeting of the American Society for Aesthetics. In that insightful presentation, Professor Harold proposed the hypothesis that what is sometimes called these days "expressivism" in ethics, the view that ethical value terms such as "right," "good," and "just," do not refer to facts about the world but express attitudes towards it, is true of aesthetic value terms such as "beautiful" and "sublime" as well. And he then went on to explore the question of how ethical attitudes and aesthetic attitudes might differ from one another.

Needless to say, ethical and aesthetic "expressivism" are the present day offspring of the old emotive theory of value. So in reading, and in framing my comments on Harold's paper I was naturally put in mind of my previous forays into ethical and aesthetic emotivism. As well, I ventured to suggest that the case was the same with ethical versus aesthetic expressivism as with ethical versus aesthetic emotivism, namely, expressivism worked better for ethics than for aesthetics, and for the same reason. Ethical expressivism could provide a plausible motive for engaging in ethical disputes, but aesthetic expressivism could not do so for aesthetic disputes. And I concluded my comments on Harold's paper by suggesting, as I had done previously in my discussion of aesthetic emotivism, that aesthetic realism, not aesthetic expressivism, could indeed provide the motive for aesthetic disputation.

But, more importantly, the thoughts that Harold's paper engendered in me did not end there. For I was now beginning to realize that the whole issue of *why* we engage in aesthetic disputes, in disputes over taste, which manifestly we do, was relatively unexplored territory in philosophy of art. And it is that territory that I then resolved to explore.

We are, indisputably, disputatious animals. Our lives are filled with episodes in which we attempt to bring others round to our way of thinking, and they us to theirs. We seem compelled, as it were, to seek from others acquiescence in our beliefs or our attitudes. And we engage in disputation, in argument, as well as in other forms of persuasion, to bring agreement about.

Sometimes it is obvious why someone would wish to persuade someone else of his belief, or bring her around to share his attitude. Sometimes, however, it is not. And it is my contention here that it is *not* obvious why we *should* wish to persuade others to share what I shall call, broadly speaking, our "aesthetic" beliefs or attitudes. But, furthermore, it seems clear to me that, nevertheless, we *do* so wish, as is made quite evident by the widespread existence, both past and present, of vigorous, persistent, and on occasion heated aesthetic disputation among commentators on the arts as well as among the general public. Thus it appears to me we are faced with a classic kind of philosophical dilemma. There seems no apparent reason why we *should* dispute about taste in the arts, and in beauty, yet ample evidence that we *do*. It is this philosophical dilemma that I wish to explore in the present book.

As with many of my other writings, this one begins with, and is deeply indebted to eighteenth-century philosophers, and particularly, Francis Hutcheson, David Hume, and Immanuel Kant. For it is in the Enlightenment that the *modern* discipline of aesthetics and philosophy of art begins. And the problem I am engaged with here seems to me embedded in that formative period in the discipline to such a degree that starting my discussion anywhere else would be tantamount to an act of intellectual dishonesty as well as intellectual suicide. Like so much else in contemporary philosophy, my problem begins in earnest in the early modern period. And so it is there that I will not only begin, but return to frequently as the need arises.

That being said, I will just append the caveat that the present book is not by any means meant to be an essay in the history of aesthetics and philosophy of art but, I hope, a contribution to the present "state of the art."

When, however, I was confronted with the daunting prospect of such a project as I have just now described, I was faced with a difficult choice. To pursue it to the bitter end, and reach a really definite conclusion with regard to all the forms of what I have been calling "aesthetic realism" would have constituted an undertaking which, at the present stage of my life, I realized I would in all probability never live to complete. I therefore decided on the present, far from thorough set of reflections on why we dispute about taste, and a tentative defense of "artistic realism" as an answer, strong in "suggestions," but woefully weak in argument.

Thus, what I have hoped to do here is not to thoroughly survey the relatively unexplored philosophical territory that I have the temerity to think I have discovered but, at least, to have opened the territory, as it were, for others to explore in the future. If I have succeeded in instigating such an exploration on the part of others, I will consider my time to have been well spent.

That having been said, it is necessary, and a pleasant task, for me to thank two anonymous readers for Oxford University Press, without whose penetrating comments, criticism, and suggestions for improvement this book would be a far poorer one. But needless to say, any defects in argument or exposition still therein are my responsibility alone.

And it remains now to thank, yet again, Peter Momtchiloff, of the Press, for his generous support and help in seeing through the arduous path to publication of another of my books. His faith in my work over the years has never wavered, even when mine has.

PETER KIVY

New York
Winter 2014

"Euclid alone has looked on beauty bare."
Edna St. Vincent Millay

1

Hume's Dilemma

The Latin maxim, *De gustibus non disputandum est*, to which the title of this book of course alludes, is customarily translated into English as "There is no disputing about taste," or something to that effect, needless to say the "taste" referred to being taste in things aesthetic, works of art principally but not by any means exclusively. The French have it as *A chacun son goût*, which is to say, "To each his own taste." What exactly do these old saws connote?

"There is no disputing about taste," if taken descriptively, and not as an admonition, seems to be expressing the obviously false proposition that, in fact, people do not argue about matters aesthetic. For in fact they *do*. So, understood more charitably, we should take it, perhaps, to be expressing the proposition, shared by many, that it is pointless, fruitless, even irrational to dispute about matters of taste because there are no "objective" criteria by which such disputes might be settled, as there are in matters of "fact." (Isn't that what it *means*, when someone says, "Well, that is merely a matter of taste"?) Or, as the logical positivists would have put it (and more about them anon), there might well be altercations over matters aesthetic; however they are not, strictly speaking, "disputes"— rather, "pseudo-disputes," disputes in appearance only, since a dispute, correctly understood, can only be a disagreement over matters of fact, which aesthetic disputes, falsely so-called, clearly are not, since there are no objective criteria available to settle them: in other words, no aesthetic "facts." On the logical positivist interpretation, then, *De gustibus non disputandum est* is a literally true descriptive statement, as aesthetic "altercations," which there *are*, do not qualify as disputes.

The French expression has, if I may be permitted to put it thus, a particularly "French" flavor to it, apart from the obvious fact that it is in French. One can almost perceive in the maxim, "To each his own taste," that distinctive, dismissive Gallic shrug of the shoulders signaling complete unconcern. "To each his own taste" seems to be merely a special case of familiar French tolerance: in fact, as a special case of "To each his own vice." It is not so much that disputing over taste is fruitless or irrational: it is just bad manners, a breach of etiquette— indeed, it is *in bad taste*.

It should be clear that on any reasonable interpretation of either *De gustibus non disputandum est* or *A chacun son goût*, both assume that there *is*, in fact, arguing over taste, at least in the minimal sense of people trying to convince or persuade other people to their belief (if it *is* a belief) or their attitude (if attitude rather than belief is what is at stake). For what each seems to be asserting, one way or another, is that such discourse *shouldn't* be indulged in, which, of course, implies that it *is* in fact indulged in.

The two philosophers in the early modern period who first, I think, brought the disputative phenomenology (if I may so describe it) of aesthetic discourse to our philosophical attention were Hume and Kant. And there is ample evidence that the latter was well acquainted with the writings of the former on this regard.

In his essay, "The Sceptic" (1742), Hume argued vigorously for the mind-dependence of beauty. "If we can depend upon any principle which we learn from philosophy," he wrote in that place, "this, I think, may be considered as certain and undoubted, that there is nothing, in itself, valuable or despicable, desirable or hateful, beautiful or deformed; but that these attributes arise from the particular constitution and fabric of human sentiment and affection."[1] And again: "when the mind... pronounces one object deformed and odious, another beautiful and amiable... those qualities are not really in the objects, but belong entirely to the sentiment of that mind which blames or praises."[2] Furthermore, with direct reference to the arts, Hume writes that "the beauty [of a poem], properly speaking, lies not in the poem, but in the sentiment or taste of the reader."[3]

Yet, Hume soon backs off from this extreme "subjectivism" by averring that "There is something approaching to principles in mental taste; and critics can reason and dispute more plausibly than cooks or

---

[1] David Hume, "The Sceptic," in Hume, *Essays, Moral, Political, and Literary* (Oxford: Oxford University Press, 1971), p. 164.

[2] Hume, "The Sceptic," *Essays*, p. 165.   [3] Hume, "The Sceptic," *Essays*, p. 168.

perfumers."[4] But no sooner has he made this concession than he makes recantation: "We may observe, however, that this uniformity among human kind hinders not, but that there is a considerable diversity in the sentiments of beauty and worth."[5] And, further, when it comes to disputation in such matters, "You have not even any single argument beyond your own taste, which you can employ in your behalf; and to your antagonist his particular taste will always appear a more convincing argument."[6] As Kant succinctly puts Hume's position on this regard in "The Sceptic": "Thus although critics, as Hume says, are able to reason more plausibly than cooks, they must still share the same fate."[7]

What are we to make of this? On the one hand, Hume is casting considerable doubt on there being any point at all in disputes over the beautiful; for in such a dispute "If you be wise, each of you will allow that the other may be in the right."[8] (In the *right*?) But on the other hand, he admits by implication that there *are* such disputes and that "critics can reason and dispute more plausibly than cooks or perfumers." What makes a critic's reasoning and disputation more "plausible" than a cook's, if it is Hume's view, as Kant puts it, that the critics "must still share the same fate" as the cooks? And, more important for our purposes, if critics *do* share the fate of cooks, *why* should we engage in disputes over the merits of art works, which we manifestly *do*, both the laity and the critics, where we manifestly seldom do, over the merits of meals?

Hume offers no explanation in "The Sceptic" for the prevalence of disputation concerning the beautiful, and so forth, in art, our major concern here. Nor does he tell us, as I have said, what makes such disputes more "plausible" than those of cooks. But in a later essay, much commented upon these days, "Of the Standard of Taste" (1757), we are provided with more information on the whole matter of taste, that warrants our attention.

I am not concerned, at this stage of the argument, with going over in detail Hume's account of the standard of taste.[9] But what I am

---

[4] Hume, "The Sceptic," *Essays*, p. 165.   [5] Hume, "The Sceptic," *Essays*, p. 165.

[6] Hume, "The Sceptic," *Essays*, p. 165.

[7] Immanuel Kant, *Critique of Aesthetic Judgement*, trans. James Creed Meredith (Oxford: Clarendon Press, 1911), p. 141 (§34).

[8] Hume, "The Sceptic," *Essays*, pp. 165–6.

[9] On this, see Peter Kivy, *The Seventh Sense: Francis Hutcheson and Eighteenth-Century British Aesthetics* (2nd ed. Oxford: Clarendon Press, 2003), Chapters VIII, XIII, XVI, and XVII.

particularly interested in right now is what light the essay on taste can (or cannot) shed on the question of *why* there should be disputing about taste *at all*.

In "Of the Standard of Taste" Hume reiterates the view expressed in "The Sceptic" that "Beauty is no quality in things themselves; it exists merely in the mind which contemplates them."[10] But if this is so, then: "To seek the real beauty, or real deformity, is as fruitless an inquiry, as to pretend to ascertain the real sweet or bitter; and the proverb has justly determined it to be fruitless to dispute concerning taste."[11] Furthermore, Hume continues: "It is very natural and even quite necessary to extend this axiom to mental, as well as bodily taste,"[12] which is to say, matters of art as well as to matters of cookery.

But as those familiar with the essay on taste will know, Hume recognized that the common sense notion encapsulated in *De gustibus non disputandum est* is directly opposed by another, endorsed as well by common sense (or so Hume thinks). It is the notion that sometimes there can be no doubt who is the better artist or what the better artwork. And in such cases, as Hume put the point: "The principle of the natural equality of tastes is then totally forgot, and while we admit it on some occasions, where the objects seem near an equality, it seems an extravagant paradox, or rather a palpable absurdity, where objects so disproportioned are compared together."[13]

But if there *are* cases where it is *obvious*, at least to some suitably identifiable group, suitably "qualified" group would be begging an important question that needs to be argued for, then we seem drawn to the conclusion that members of such a group would be prepared to defend the obvious against those who do not perceive it. So we are driven yet again to the recognition that there *are* disputes about taste, and as yet no explanation of *why* there should be. Why should I care to convince someone that, to use Hume's example, Milton is a better poet than Ogilby?[14] Let him value Ogilby. What is it to *me*?

---

[10] Hume, "Of the Standard of Taste," *Essays*, p. 234.
[11] Hume, "Of the Standard of Taste," *Essays*, p. 235.
[12] Hume, "Of the Standard of Taste," *Essays*, p. 235.
[13] Hume, "Of the Standard of Taste," *Essays*, p. 235.
[14] Hume, "Of the Standard of Taste," *Essays*, p. 235.

Perhaps, though, we will be able to extract an answer to this question from Hume's essay on taste by understanding more fully just what Hume thinks the nature of beauty *is* and, therefore, just what I would be trying to convince someone *of* if I were trying to convince him of the obvious: that Milton is a better poet than Ogilby; or, more specifically, that this poem of Milton's is orders of magnitude better than that poem of Ogilby's.

In "The Sceptic," what might escape the casual reader's notice is a long footnote in which Hume analogizes the beautiful to what the eighteenth-century British empiricists had come to call, after Locke, the "secondary qualities." Of these, as we have seen, the bitter and the sweet were alluded to in the essay on taste as having the same ontology as the deformed and the beautiful. But in "The Sceptic," as well as in "Of the Standard of Taste," Hume is far more interested, and with good reason, as we shall see, in analogizing the ontology of the beautiful to that of colors. Furthermore, in "The Sceptic," as in other of Hume's more important and better known works, moral qualities too figure in the analogy—a point that will be returned to at length later on.

In the footnote to which I allude, then, Hume undertakes to "remind" his reader that, as has been "fully proved in modern times, . . . the tastes and colours, and all other sensible qualities, lie not in the bodies, but merely in the senses. The case is the same," he continues, "with beauty and deformity, virtue and vice." But Hume is, as well, anxious to reassure his reader that "This doctrine [of secondary qualities], however, takes off no more from the reality of the latter qualities than from that of the former; nor need it give any umbrage to critics or moralists." And that he is thinking far more of the analogy to colors here than to taste of the palate is made very clear in the remark which follows: "Though colours were allowed to lie only in the eye, would dyers or painters ever be less regarded or esteemed?" And Hume therefore concludes his thought: "There is a sufficient uniformity in the senses and feelings of mankind, to make all these qualities the object of art and reasoning, and to have the greatest influence on life and manners."[15]

Furthermore, that Hume has colors mainly in mind when he analogizes the ontology of beauty to that of the secondary qualities is made all

---

[15] Hume, "The Sceptic," *Essays*, p. 168n.

the more apparent in the essay on taste, where he writes: "If, in the sound state of the organ, there be an entire or a considerable uniformity of sentiment among men, we may there derive an idea of the perfect beauty; in like manner as the appearance of objects in daylight, to the eye of a man in health, is denominated their true and real colours, even when colour is allowed to be merely a phantasm of the senses."[16]

The missing term in the analogy, so far, is what would correspond, in matters of aesthetic taste, to "the eye of a man in health" in matters of color perception. Readers of the essay on taste will know, of course, that it is what Hume calls there, in one place, "the true judge in the finer arts," who is characterized, Hume thinks, by "strong sense, united to delicate sentiment, improved by practice, perfected by comparison, and cleared of all prejudice." Hume concludes: "the joint verdict of such, wherever they are to be found, is the true standard of taste and beauty,"[17] as is "the eye of the man in health" the true standard of what color a necktie is.

Now there ought, it would seem, be some close connection between what one thinks the ontology of the beautiful is, and what one thinks would be the instance or reason for engaging in disputes over it. And in this regard Hume does indeed give at least a hint, in adducing an incident from *Don Quixote*, much discussed in the Hume literature on his aesthetics. According to the story, told by Sancho Panza, two of his kinsman, renowned for their delicate taste in wine, were asked to sample a keg, and make a judgment. Each of them declared favorably for the vintage except that one detected a slight taste of leather, the other of iron.

You cannot imagine how much they were both ridiculed for their judgment. But who laughed in the end? On emptying the hogshead, there was found at the bottom an old key with a leathern thong tied to it.[18]

So how are we to understand the moral of this tale?

First of all, there is a disagreement about how the wine tastes. Sancho's kinsmen say it tastes of leather and iron. Their detractors say it does not. But so far it is not a genuine disagreement. For a more accurate way of describing the situation is to say that the wine tastes like leather and wine *to* the kinsmen and not *to* their detractors. However, for there to be a

---

[16] Hume, "Of the Standard of Taste," *Essays*, pp. 238–9.
[17] Hume, "Of the Standard of Taste," *Essays*, p. 247.
[18] Hume, "Of the Standard of Taste," *Essays*, p. 240.

genuine disagreement one of the parties has to be saying p, the other not-p. And, clearly, that is not the case here; p and not -p cannot both be true, whereas "It taste like leather to Peter" and "It doesn't taste like leather to Paul" can both be true, whether or not the hogshead contains a key and a thong.

The question, then, might be framed in this way. Are Sancho's kinsmen *justified* in tasting leather and iron in the wine? Is the taste *really* there? But what could it possibly mean to say that the *taste* of leather and iron are *really* there if, as Hume puts it, such secondary qualities are really "a phantasm of the senses"?

If finding the key and the thong in the hogshead "proves" that the taste of leather and iron are *really* there, Sancho's kinsmen right, their detractors wrong, according to Hume, then he must mean something like this. That the key and the thong are *really* there is not in dispute: *that* is a matter of fact. Furthermore, their presence is agreed upon by the disputants as providing an adequate explanation of how "something" got into the wine from the key and thong that produced the taste of leather and iron on the palates of Sancho's kinsmen—an explanation, presumably, ruling out the possibility of the taste being caused by some quirk of the kinsmen's psychology or physiology. The explanation, one presumes, would be in the form of some empirically founded law-like generalization about the presence of leather and iron in the wine introducing "something" into it that would be detected by sensitive enough perceivers as the taste of leather and iron on their palates.

Is there an analogue to the thong and the key in judgments of the beautiful and the like? Hume, needless to say, thinks there is. First of all, Hume thinks that there are general principles of correct composition in the arts, founded, *a posteriori*, upon what has been found over the centuries to gratify in matters aesthetic and artistic: "general rules of beauty . . . drawn from established models, and from the observation of what pleases or displeases, when presented singly and in a high degree." Furthermore, Hume avers: "To produce these general rules or avowed patterns of composition, is like finding the key with the leathern thong, which justified the verdict of Sancho's kinsmen, and confounded those pretended judges who had condemned them."[19]

---

[19] Hume, "Of the Standard of Taste," *Essays*, p. 240.

How so? How do we convince a recalcitrant critic that he is mistaken over a question of artistic merit with this, as it were, aesthetic thong and key? Hume explains:

> But when we show him an avowed principle of art; when we illustrate this principle with examples, whose operation, from his own particular taste, he acknowledges to be conformable to the principle; when we prove that the same principle may be applied to the present case, where he did not perceive or feel its influence: he must conclude, upon the whole, that the fault lies with himself, and that he wants the delicacy which is requisite to make him sensible of every beauty and every blemish in any composition or discourse.[20]

Note well that in both cases—the wine tasting and the art tasting—the end in view seems to be solely to bring your opponent to his knees: to have the last laugh, as Hume describes the triumph of Sancho Panza's kinsmen.

But the question persists. Why should Hume's "true judge" *care* if he gets the last laugh? Why should he have the slightest interest in convincing someone who does *not* perceive a blemish in a work of art that he does perceive that the blemish is "really there" (whatever, in the event, that turns out to mean)? Or, in other words, *why* are there aesthetic disputes? Hume does not seem to have an answer, although he obviously believes such disputes occur. Perhaps he thought no answer was necessary: that it was simply a brute, unexplainable fact of life.

If critics do not just want to win arguments but to serve some useful purpose, then it might seem reasonable to believe that their principal motive in disputation is some kind of benevolent one: to help enable others to perceive in works of art what they perceive in them, hence to enjoy in works of art what they enjoy in them, and what their adversaries are unable to enjoy because unable, without the critic's help, to perceive. The motive of the critics, then, is, quite simply, to increase world happiness (in their own small way): a reasonable enough motive, after all, to explain and justify aesthetic disputation.

The problem is, as Hume's example graphically demonstrates, critics *also* delight in revealing the blemishes in works of art; the faults in composition, and so forth. And in getting their adversaries to perceive these faults and blemishes they would be *decreasing* rather than

---

[20] Hume, "Of the Standard of Taste," *Essays*, p. 241.

augmenting their adversaries' enjoyment of works of art. But why, it can reasonably then be asked, should I want to spoil someone's pleasure in an artwork by discovering its faults to her? If I am motivated, as a critic. by *benevolence*, I should want to leave her alone; to rejoice in her enjoyment of a work I *cannot* enjoy because I perceive it as faulty. If I am motivated by *self-interest*, there is no reason to convince her of its faults. If I am motivated by *benevolence*, there is good reason *not* to convince her of its faults. And, like Bishop Butler, I do not recognize pure *malevolence*, absent of self-interest, as a possible motive. So we are left, so far, with no reason to believe there *should* be disputing about taste, and ample evidence that there *is*.

This might seem a strange conclusion. And I shall return to that aspect of it that rejects *benevolence* as a motive for critical disputation later on. But for now we can conclude at least this: Hume believes that there *is* in fact disputing about taste. And he believes as well that sometimes one of the parties to such a dispute is right, the other wrong. But, so far as I can see, he provides no explicit explanation for why such disputes should occur, as manifestly they *do*.

But in matters of aesthetics, as elsewhere, Hume awoke Kant from his dogmatic slumber. So perhaps we may find in Kant what we cannot seem to find in Hume: an explanation, or motive, if you will, for disputing over questions of aesthetic taste. So to Kant's animadversions on the subject I now turn my attention.

2

A Ground Common to All

My readers will perhaps be pleased to know that I have no intention of getting deeply into the complexities of serious Kant interpretation, a task I am singularly unqualified for. What I am interested in is understanding, on what I take to be a common sense level, what Kant is saying about, if I may so put it, the "phenomenology" and *raison d'être* of what *we* would call "aesthetic" discourse, and what Kant calls the "pure judgments of taste," which is to say, judgments of the beautiful.

Kant, like Hume, as many of my readers will know, thought that when we call something "beautiful" it is in virtue of its producing a certain kind of pleasurable feeling in us. In sharp contrast to present day usage, Kant called *all* judgments so based on *feeling* in the perceiver "aesthetic" judgments, thus making judgments to the effect that caviar is "delicious" or "disgusting," as well as judgments that an artwork is "beautiful" or the opposite, "aesthetic" judgments. What kind of "speech act" such "aesthetic" judgments might be, in particular, judgments of the beautiful, and other of what *we* would call "aesthetic" judgments, I will get to by and by. But here I turn to the "phenomenology" of aesthetic judgments and their *raison d'être*.

In §7 of the *Critique of Aesthetic Judgment* Kant contrasts the judgment of the "agreeable" with judgments of beauty. "With regard to the agreeable . . . ," Kant avers, "the axiom holds good: *Every one has his own taste.*" But things are different with regard to judgments of the beautiful. When one makes such a judgment, "He judges not merely for himself, but for all men, and then speaks of beauty as if it were a property of things," or, in other words, "he says the *thing* is beautiful." Of others, "he *demands* . . . agreement." And, furthermore, "He blames them if they judge differently, and denies them taste, which he still requires of them as something they ought to have; and to this extent it is not open to men to say: Every one has his own taste."[1]

What are we to make of Kant's claims here? Not surprisingly, it is not altogether clear.

Let me begin with the obvious (and I believe uncontentious) observation that Kant is, among other things, making an empirical observation about how people in general ordinarily behave when making judgments of the beautiful, to wit, they demand agreement from others, they blame others who do not agree with them, they speak as if beauty were a property of things and not merely a subjective reaction we have to them.

But what is uncertain in these descriptions is whether Kant means to suggest by them that people argue with those who do not judge beautiful what *they* judge beautiful for the purpose of bringing them round: in other words, bringing about agreement. For it is perfectly compatible with my demanding agreement from others, expecting agreement from others, blaming others if they do not agree with me, speaking of beauty as if it were a property of things and not merely a subjective reaction we have to them, and yet walking away from the disagreement without any attempt to persuade the dissenter. For the nagging question remains as to why I should *want* to persuade others to my perceptions as to what "is" beautiful. What possible stake could I have in effecting agreement? What possible grief could I be caused by others demurring from my judgments of the beautiful? Here Kant gives us no clue.

It would, however, be a serious mistake to conclude from the above-quoted passages alone that Kant was agnostic as to whether there *is* disputing in matters of taste in the beautiful. For there are other passages that strongly suggest or, I should say rather, leave us in no real doubt that Kant thought there *is*. One such passage I have already quoted to the effect that, agreeing with Hume, Kant thought "critics . . . are able to reason more plausibly than cooks," the reasoning, one assumes, being, among other things, aimed at convincing adversaries.[2]

A far more suggestive passage is to be found in §19 of the third *Critique*, where Kant writes:

The judgement of taste exacts agreement from every one; and a person who describes something as beautiful insists that every one *ought* to give the object in

---

[1] Kant, *Critique of Aesthetic Judgement*, p. 52 (§7).
[2] See, supra, Chapter 1, note 7.

question his approval and follow suit in describing it as beautiful.... We are suitors for agreement from every one else, because we are fortified with a ground common to all.[3]

I shall return anon to the question of *what* the "ground common to all" is, according to Kant. But for the moment I am concerned with the description: "We are suitors for agreement from every one else." For to be a *suitor* is not merely to be one who requests or demands agreement but one who pleads his cause: one who doesn't just say "Marry me," but "Marry me *because* I am rich and handsome and in love." And in referring to those who make judgments of the beautiful as *suitors* for agreement from every one else Kant surely is alluding to *that* aspect of the suitor's shtick. The suitor does not just state his cause: he *presses* his suit. In other words, the person who makes a judgment of taste in the beautiful, Kant is saying, does not merely expect or demand agreement, he argues to gain it. That is what suitors do.

With that more or less settled, I want now to return to our central question of *why* we are suitors for agreement from others in judgments of the beautiful. For although Hume, as far as I can make out, did not venture an answer to this question, Kant did. And it behooves us to examine carefully what Kant had to say in this regard.

In order to fully grasp Kant's answer to the question at hand, however, we must first have at least a minimal account of how he understands judgments of the beautiful: in particular, how such a judgment can, if I may so put it, be *both* apparently "subjective" *and* apparently "objective" at the same time.

As we have already seen, Kant characterized judgments of the beautiful as "aesthetic" in *his* special sense of that term, which is to say, we experience a certain feeling upon contemplating some object or other, and the feeling elicits the response "beautiful" as referring (apparently) to that object. In Kant's words: "If we wish to discern whether anything is beautiful or not, we do not refer the representation of it to the Object by means of understanding with a view to cognition, but by means of the imagination (acting perhaps in conjunction with understanding) we refer the representation to the Subject and its feeling of pleasure or displeasure."[4]

---

[3] Kant, *Critique of Aesthetic Judgement*, p. 82 (§19).
[4] Kant, *Critique of Aesthetic Judgement*, p. 41 (§1).

But note well that although Kant attributes to imagination the role of referring the representation of beauty to the Subject, not by understanding to the Object, he adds parenthetically that the imagination in its role is "acting perhaps in conjunction with the understanding." And there is indeed no "perhaps" in the matter. For it *is* because the imagination is acting in conjunction with the understanding that although the judgment is "aesthetic" (in Kant's sense of the word), and therefore "subjective" (in our sense of the word), it is also "objective" (in our sense of the word) in that agreement is expected and solicited, unlike mere judgments of the "agreeable," "subjective" through and through, where agreement is neither expected nor solicited by argument.

Kant's seminal idea, as even casual readers of the *Critique of Aesthetic Judgment* will know, is that the pure judgment of taste, the judgment of the beautiful, must be "disinterested." As Kant puts his point, "where the question is whether something is beautiful, we do not want to know whether we, or any one else, are, or even could be, concerned with the real existence of the thing, but rather what estimate we form of it on mere contemplation."[5] Kant's notion, here, I take it, is that if we abstract from an object of perception or reflection anything that has to do with its real existence (or lack thereof), but concentrate on the mere *form* of the *appearance*, we will then *all* be taking pleasure in the very same intentional object, minus any personal interests or associations it might possess for us as a real, existent object, and that might be mistaken for the pleasure of the beautiful or the displeasure in its opposite or absence. And, furthermore, if we each achieve this attitude of disinterestedness, then we should, it might seem, all be in agreement about the beauty of the formal appearance, because we will each be devoid of any personal perturbations one way or the other.

But that does not directly follow. Disinterested perception may be a necessary condition for agreement; however, there is no reason to think it sufficient. For, after all, when your personal associations and experiences are peeled away, and mine are as well, what is left, your "core" and my "core," may be radically different: two radically different cores producing radically different feelings in contemplating the same disinterestedly perceived intentional object.

[5] Kant, *Critique of Aesthetic Judgement*, p. 43 (§2).

What more is needed, clearly, than disinterested perception, to make universal agreement in judgments of the beautiful a reasonable expectation, Kant of course must have realized, is assurance that we all do indeed have the same core. For recall, he says, "We are suitors for agreement from every one else [in the judgment of the beautiful] because *we are fortified with a ground common to all.*" What is that common ground: that common core within?

Kant's thought in this regard we already get a hint of at the outset, where, as we have seen, Kant suggests that the imagination works in conjunction with the *understanding* in judgments of the beautiful. As the thought is developed, we learn that the feeling of the beautiful emanates from what Kant terms the "free play" of the cognitive faculties of imagination and understanding, prerequisite for cognition in general. In Kant's notoriously convoluted description, "As the subjective universal communicability of the mode of representation in a judgment of taste is to subsist apart from the presupposition of any definite concept, it can be nothing else than the mental state present in the free play of imagination and understanding (so far as these are in mutual accord as is requisite for *cognition in general*)."[6] It is this free play of the imagination and the understanding, prerequisite for all human cognition, that is, in judgments of the beautiful, Kant's "ground common to all," which he later describes as a "common sense." "The judgement of taste, therefore, depends on our presupposing the existence of a common sense. (But this is not to be taken to mean some external sense, but the effect arising from the free play of our powers of cognition.)"[7]

Kant at this point has given us a description of what the ground common to all is in judgments of the beautiful, namely, the free play of the imagination and the understanding, which, when attained, as it only can be, in disinterested perception, produces that pleasurable feeling that motivates our pure judgment of taste: that motivates our pronouncing one thing or another "beautiful." What we now want to ask is *why* we should seek, be suitors for *agreement* from others in our judgments of the beautiful. And this question breaks down into two sub-questions. There is the question of *why* we want to bring others around to our judgment

---

[6] Kant, *Critique of Aesthetic Judgement*, p. 58 (§9).
[7] Kant, *Critique of Aesthetic Judgement*, p. 83 (§20).

that some thing or other is beautiful, and there is the question of *what*, if anything, *justifies* our expectation that agreement can be reached.

The answer to the second question we already have adumbrated in Kant's claim that we are suitors for agreement from others in matters of taste because there is a ground common to all. But there are complexities therein yet to be untangled; and to that task I will turn later on.

An answer to the first question, which I will tackle now, is at least hinted at, suggested, I will not say asserted outright, late in the *Critique of Aesthetic Judgment*; and Kant must be quoted here at some length to catch his drift. Kant writes:

The empirical interest in the beautiful exists only in *society*. And if we admit that the impulse to society is natural to mankind, and that the sensibility for and the propensity towards it, i.e. *sociability*, is a property essential to the requirements of man as a creature intended for society, and one, therefore, that belongs to *humanity*, it is inevitable that we should also look upon taste in the light of a faculty for estimating whatever enables us to communicate even our feeling to every one else, and hence as a means of promoting that upon which the natural inclination of every one is set.

Furthermore:

Only in society does it occur to him to be not merely a man, but a man refined after the manner of his kind (the beginning of civilization)—for that is the estimate formed of one who has the bent and turn for communicating his pleasure to others, and who is not quite satisfied with an Object unless his feeling of delight in it can be shared in communion with others.[8]

Kant's basic premise here, as he puts it, is that "the impulse to society is natural to mankind." Furthermore, getting others to share our feeling in what we find beautiful, Kant claims, is "a means of promoting that upon which the natural inclination of every one is set," namely, "*sociability*." And so, it would seem, each of us "is not quite satisfied with an Object unless his feeling of delight in it can be shared in communion with others." Or, as a recent author insightfully puts Kant's point: "One could perhaps say: you would be failing *to be* 'one of us,' and at a level of importance crucial to our being able to be and sustain being who we are."[9]

---

[8] Kant, *Critique of Aesthetic Judgement*, p. 155 (§41).
[9] Robert B. Pippin, *After the Beautiful: Hegel and the Philosophy of Pictorial Modernism* (Chicago and London: The University of Chicago Press, 2014), p. 11.

There seems, then, on Kant's view, to be a double motive, so to speak, for entering into a dispute over taste with another party. To begin with, it looks as if Kant is thinking only of cases in which someone who is experiencing the feeling of the beautiful in contemplating an object tries to "communicate" this feeling to someone else who is not experiencing it, which is to say, get *that* someone else to experience it too. He does not seem to consider the case of someone *not* experiencing the feeling of the beautiful in contemplating an object trying to get someone who *is*, or thinks he is, not to do so.

That being said, the double motivation appears to be a *benevolent* motive which ultimately cashes out in a *selfish* one. Thus, one attempts to "communicate" one's feeling of the beautiful in the contemplation of an object; one attempts to get the other to experience it as well, with the end in view of enriching or promoting "sociability." That is the benevolent motive. But one is impelled to do it, one is directly motivated to do it, because one "is not quite satisfied with an Object unless his feeling of delight can be shared in communion with others." That is the *selfish* motive, if you will: the increase in one's own delight in an object by getting someone else to share it.

Now the question that concerns me here is not about whether or not Kant is right in his claim that the communicability of the feeling of the beautiful has the beneficial socializing effect he ascribes to it. Of course one would like to think he is right. But as to how we would find out whether he is right I have no notion at all; and as I say, it is not the question at issue here.

What does concern me—it indeed lies at the center of what this book is all about—is whether Kant is right in his explanation of why we enter into disputes about taste. And in order to answer that question we will have to have some general idea as to what we mean when we say that someone performed an *action*, which disputing about taste certainly is, for such and such a reason.

Now without entering into a philosophical dispute of long standing and great complexity, that would lead us far astray of the topic, I will simply take this very general statement, of a recent author, as to what it would mean for someone to act "for reasons." She writes: "whenever an agent acts for reasons, the agent, in some sense, takes certain considerations to settle the question of whether so to act, therein intends so to act, and executes that intention in action."[10] And we can now ask, with this

---

[10] Pamela Hieronymi, "Reasons for Action," *Proceedings of the Aristotelian Society*, New Series, 111 (2011), p. 421.

general characterization of what we *are* asking, whether Kant is correct in his apparent contention that whenever an agent performs the action of trying to convince another of the correctness of his judgment of taste, the action of trying to bring the other to experience the feeling of beauty in contemplating the object he is feeling in contemplating it, he does so with the intention to "socialize" the other, and, in so doing, increase his own satisfaction, or decrease his own dissatisfaction by shared communion with the other in the feeling of beauty. I find the claim hard to credit. It is a beautiful thought, perhaps. And perhaps someone, sometimes, enters into a dispute over taste for the reasons Kant suggests. But as a general characterization of the sole motivating reason for such disputes it seems highly implausible.

But, it may be responded, perhaps the implausibility felt in this regard is due to our interpreting Kant as saying that we *consciously* entertain as our end in view what he describes as the reason for entering into disputes over the beautiful, whereas what he is really saying is that it is some kind of unconscious underlying motive or "cause." Again, however, this claim strikes me as both without real foundation and highly implausible.

But that having been said, it can also be said, on Kant's behalf, that he did recognize, as Hume apparently did not, the necessity for an explanation of why we engage in dispute over beauty and the other merits (or demerits) of art objects—what our "intention in action" in so doing might be. That we *do* is manifest. Why we do seems a question philosophers seldom address, which is why I am addressing it in this book.

Moving on, now, to the second, related question, given that we *do* enter into disputes in which we try to bring others around to agreement with us in matters of taste, the related question is *why* we feel we can succeed in bringing about such agreement. What justifies us in thinking that?

As we have seen, Kant's answer is, in the most general terms, that we seek to elicit agreement from others, with confidence that agreement can be achieved, because we believe "we are fortified with a ground common to all." Kant was not, indeed, the first philosopher of his century to make such a claim. It is implicit in Hume's essay on taste, which Kant knew well. And it is made much of in Lord Kames' highly influential *Elements of Criticism*, of 1761, which Kant undoubtedly knew, as it was published in German translation the following year.[11]

---

[11] I am indebted to Paul Guyer for this information.

Thus, Kames writes in this regard, that: "With respect to the common nature of man in particular, we have a conviction that it is invariable not less than universal." Furthermore: "This conviction of a common nature or standard . . . ," he continues, "accounts . . . for the conception we have of a right and a wrong sense or taste in the fine arts."[12]

Kant exhibits two contrasting ways of formulating this general principle of "a ground common to all." In the first, which I have quoted more than once, he says: "We are suitors for agreement from every one else [in matters of taste] because we are fortified with a ground common to all." In the second, which I have also quoted, he has it that: "The judgement of taste, therefore, depends on our presupposing the existence of a common sense." He adds—and this may be crucial to our understanding of what he is saying—that: "Only under the *presupposition*, I repeat, of such a common sense, are we able to lay down a judgement of taste."[13]

I am assuming, however, that even though Kant expresses the principle of the common ground in two contrasting ways, they are to be interpreted as expressing the basically same thought. And this is what I take that thought to be.

When Kant says we are suitors for agreement from others in matters of taste *because* we are "fortified" by a ground common to all, I take him to be saying that we feel justified in so doing, that we think we can succeed in so doing, because we actually do believe we share the relevant common ground. And did we not believe that, we would not press our suit, as we do not in matters of the merely agreeable.

This is brought out, I think, most explicitly in Kant's second way of making his point, where, as he puts it, "The judgement of taste, therefore, depends on our presupposing the existence of a common sense." And again: "Only under the presupposition, I repeat, of a common sense, are we able to lay down a judgement of taste."

We "presuppose" a "common sense"; it is *our presupposing*. Who is this "we"? Well I think it pretty clear that it is the "we" who make judgments of taste: it is "our" presupposition that there is a "common sense," "a ground common to all." And we must be acting under that

[12] Henry Home [Lord Kames], *Elements of Criticism* (6th ed. Edinburgh, 1785), vol. II, pp. 491–2.
[13] Kant, *Critique of Aesthetic Judgement*, p. 83 (§20). My italics.

presupposition because, as Kant has claimed at the outset, when we make a judgment of taste, which is to say, a judgment of the beautiful, we, in so doing, are suitors for agreement from others and expect it. For without that assumption, without *believing* in a common sense, a ground common to all, in matters of taste, there would be no point in seeking agreement, arguing for it, and no grounds for thinking we could achieve it by argument (or any other form of persuasion).

Two caveats in this regard now must be entered.

First, as Charles Landesman puts it, Kant, in that section of the *Critique of Pure Reason* called "The Paralogisms of Pure Reason," seems to have been claiming "that 'I think' accompanies every [mental] representation." Or, in other words: "He seemed to believe that it is a necessary truth that whenever a person thinks that A, whatever A may be, he also thinks 'I think that A.'"[14] That being the case, it would also seem to follow that whenever, in Kant's view, someone makes a judgment of taste, he not only thinks that we are fortified with a ground common to all but thinks that he thinks it. Put another way, we must be consciously entertaining the thought that we are fortified with a ground common to all whenever we try to persuade someone to our taste.

But the view seems highly implausible. For to begin with, as a general principle, it results, as Landesman points out, in an infinite regress, in the following way. If I think that A, I must think that I think that A. And if I think that I think that A, then I must think that I think that I think that A.... And so *in infinitum*.

But in any event, with regard to the particular case in question here, it appears highly unlikely that whenever someone attempts to persuade someone else to his taste, he always has consciously before his mind his belief that he is fortified with a ground common to all, which is to say, that he not only believes it; he thinks he believes it. (It is certainly not the case with me.) Far more plausible, I would think, is the view that whenever we attempt to persuade others to our own taste, we are *implicitly* assuming that we are fortified with a ground common to all. As Landesman puts it, in regard to the general case, we are "to disconnect representational consciousness from self-consciousness. Although one

---

[14] Charles Landesman, *Leibniz's Mill: A Challenge to Materialism* (Notre Dame: University of Notre Dame Press, 2011), p. 30.

may be conscious of one's own act of thought, it is not necessary that one be conscious of it."[15]

Thus I will put what I take to be a distinctly un-Kantian construction on Kant's notion that in trying to persuade others to our judgments of taste we presuppose a common sense, a ground common to all. I will take it to mean not that we are (always) consciously aware of this presupposition when we make judgments of taste and argue for them but that it is implicit in our action--"internalized," if you will. We believe it though we are not (always) consciously aware *that* we believe it, much in the way, for example, I drive my car under the presupposition that other drivers follow the same "rules of the road" as I do, even though while I am driving I am not occurrently conscious of this necessary presupposition. And this brings we to my second caveat.

I believe Kant's view, suitably modified, as I have done, is spot on: right on the money. In entering into disputes over matters of taste, we endeavor to convince others to share our taste. And we could not hope to succeed—it would be fruitless for us to try—unless we believed that we and our opponents were fortified with a common ground. I do not say that it must be the common ground Kant thought it was: the free play of the imagination and the understanding. I do not, as a matter of fact, believe that is what it is. But I do think it is correctly described as "a ground common to all." Nor do I think we can make aesthetic disputes intelligible (in our sense of "aesthetic") without our assuming a ground common to all. Kant was right.

But—and here comes the second caveat—this hardly is a presupposition unique to aesthetic disputation. It would seem difficult to understand why I should attempt to convince anyone of *anything* with any hope of success unless I presupposed that we shared a common ground of the appropriate kind, although, of course, what kind of common ground I am presupposing depends upon what it is I am trying to convince the other of. Thus, if I try to convince a scientific colleague that my theory of planetary formation is correct, I naturally do so under the unspoken and (most of the time) un-thought-of assumption that we share as a common ground the current methods of planetary science and, needless to say, *rationality* (however that elusive concept may be

---

[15] Landesman, *Leibniz's Mill*, p. 30.

understood). And even if I am a charlatan, attempting to convince my mark of something I know to be false, all of the techniques of rhetoric and propagandistic persuasion that I employ I employ under the presupposition of a ground common to all, or there would be no reason for me to believe that these time-honored (or dishonored) means of making the worse cause appear the better will work.

So Kant was right, and right about three things.

Kant was right that when we make judgments of the beautiful we expect agreement from others and try by persuasion, in one way or another, to bring others around to our taste. We do not just walk away from disputes about taste.

Kant was right, as well, that when we make judgments of the beautiful, and attempt persuasion, the only way such behavior can seem plausible, and possible of success, is in assuming that when we perform such actions we do so under the presupposition of a ground common to all, although we need not, nor do I, accept Kant's account of what the nature of that common ground is.

Kant was right, finally, in his recognition that an explanation is wanted for why we feel the need to persuade others to our taste, although, again, we need not, nor do I, accept Kant's explanation. So we are left, still, with the central theme of this book: the reason or motive for (in our sense of the word) *aesthetic* disputation. Where might we find it?

A logical first place to look would be ethical discourse. For there is a long tradition, dating at least as far back as the eighteenth century, the cradle of modern aesthetics, of comparing ethical with aesthetic judgment. And to that comparison, and its possible implications, I now turn my attention.

3

The Beautiful versus the Good (in the Eighteenth Century)

I begin with a truism. In the comparison between ethical and aesthetic judgments the result is either to make out that they are, in principle, the same, or that they are, in principle, quite different. And this seems to have been the way things went right from the get go: the early eighteenth century, where we can date the origin of modern philosophical aesthetics. So let's begin our examination of the comparison between the ethical and the aesthetic at the beginning—or, at least, where I understand the beginning to have begun: in Francis Hutcheson's *An Inquiry into the Original of our Ideas of Beauty and Virtue*, of 1725.

Hutcheson's *Inquiry* consists, actually, of two separate but closely related treatises, the first, "Beauty, Order, Harmony, Design," and the second, "Moral Good and Evil." And note well that the order is first a treatise on what *we* would call aesthetics, the second on moral philosophy. The reason for this order, I think, is clear, and philosophically significant. For Hutcheson's major concern was to argue that moral judgments are judgments of sense, of "subjective" feeling, not reason. And his strategy for preparing his readers for this disturbing, seemingly skeptical position in moral philosophy was to first remind his readers, so to speak, that this was not an unfamiliar or disturbing position to take with regard to judgments of the beautiful which, after all, have behind them the old and familiar adage that *beauty is in the eye of the beholder*. Thus Hutcheson was working his passage from the more familiar, and less shocking idea that judgments of the beautiful are based upon our subjective feelings to the far less familiar and, indeed, uncongenial idea that moral judgments are so based as well.

Of beauty, Hutcheson writes, close to the outset of the "Treatise Concerning Beauty, Order, Harmony, Design": "Let it be observ'd that in the following Papers, the Word *Beauty* is taken for *the Idea rais'd in us*, and a *Sense* of Beauty for *our Power of receiving this Idea*."[1] Furthermore, Hutcheson makes it clear, early on, that his model for the idea of beauty within us is that of the Lockean secondary qualities. For he writes that by beauty "is not understood any Quality suppos'd to be in the Object, which should of itself be beautiful, without relation to any Mind which perceives it: For Beauty, like other Names of sensible Ideas, properly denotes the *Perception* of some Mind; so *Cold, Hot, Sweet, Bitter*, denote the Sensations in our Minds, to which there is no Resemblance in the Objects, which excite the Ideas in us, however we generally imagine otherwise."[2]

Thus, having reminded the reader, if you will, of the common, though not universal notion that beauty is no quality in objects but, rather, a sensation, an "idea" (in the Lockean parlance) that objects may elicit in the perceiver, and, furthermore, having this common sense, "subjective" notion of the beautiful as merely a special case of the Lockean notion of "secondary qualities," Hutcheson has prepared the reader to take the next, more difficult step with him, and see moral qualities in the same light. And Hutcheson makes that proposal straightaway, in the very first sentence of the second treatise: "An Inquiry Concerning Moral Good and Evil," with no preamble whatever. "The Word MORAL GOOD-NESS, in this Treatise," he writes," denotes our Idea of *some Quality apprehended in Actions, which procures Approbation, attended with Desire of the Agent's Happiness. MORAL EVIL denotes our Idea of a contrary Quality which excites Condemnation or Dislike*."[3]

Now it is not my intention at this juncture to go into any further detail with regard either to Hutcheson's aesthetic or ethical theory, although I will be returning to Hutcheson and the eighteenth century later on.[4] My point here is only that at what I take to be the outset of modern aesthetic philosophy, Hutcheson made the comparison between aesthetic and moral judgments, putting them both, as a result, on the same epistemic and ontological footing. Furthermore, less than ten years later, in the first

---

[1] Francis Hutcheson, *An Inquiry into the Original of our Ideas of Beauty and Virtue* (4th ed. London, 1738), p. 7.

[2] Hutcheson, *An Inquiry into the Original of our Ideas of Beauty and Virtue*, p. 14.

[3] Hutcheson, *An Inquiry into the Original of our Ideas of Beauty and Virtue*, p. 105.

[4] For a thorough exposition of my views on Hutcheson's aesthetic theory, and its influence in eighteenth-century Britain, see Peter Kivy, *The Seventh Sense*.

"rationalist" critique of Hutcheson's "sentimentalist" value theory, John Balguy made the same comparison, and came out, in his first writings on the subject, with a very different conclusion.

Balguy's first characterization of the distinction between judgments of the morally good and judgments of the beautiful is likely to seem extremely puzzling to the present day reader because *both* are being construed as *moral* judgments; which is to say, both are being construed as judgments with regard to the rightness of actions. Balguy begins: "*Virtue,* or moral goodness, may be considered under the Notion of *Pulchrum* or *Honestum.*" And he goes on, "while every rational Creature clearly and uniformly perceives, in all ordinary Cases, what is *fit,* and *just,* and *right*; many Men have little or no Perception of that *Beauty* in Actions, with which others are wonderfully charmed."[5]

It will not, or should not disturb the reader familiar with the eighteenth-century British moralists to find Balguy using "beautiful" in a moral sense. To call an action or character "beautiful" was, in a sense of beautiful that has now fallen into disuse, to bestow upon it moral approval. But what does, and should seem odd is Balguy's distinction between the moral sense of "beautiful" and the moral senses of "fit" and "just" and "right." For it would seem that to call an action "beautiful" in the eighteenth-century moral sense just *is* to call it "right" or "just" or "fit"; and if someone saw an action as right or just or fit he would, *ipso facto,* perceive it as beautiful (in the moral sense). I shall not delve into this puzzlement here, as I have done so elsewhere, and, in any case, it is not relevant to present concerns.[6]

What *does* concern me here is Balguy's contrast between judgments of the beautiful and judgments of the right and just, ignoring the puzzling fact that they are all, as Balguy is considering them at this point, moral judgments. For, arguing from the (by then) familiar claim that there is general agreement over whether or not something is just or right, and wide-spread disagreement over whether something is beautiful or not, Balguy draws the conclusion, albeit a tentative conclusion, that, in

---

[5] John Balguy, *The Foundations of Moral Goodness: or, A Further Inqiury into the Original of our Idea of Virtue* (4th ed.), in Balguy, *A Collection of Tracts Moral and Theological* (London, 1734), p. 60.

[6] On this, see Peter Kivy, "John Balguy and the Sense of Beauty: A Rational Realist in the Age of Sentiment," *Enlightenment and Dissent,* No. 23 (2004–7).

perceiving beauty, as opposed to rightness or justness, "the Mind ...
must be looked upon, not as *intelligent*, but *sensible*."[7] Or, in other words,
in his comparison of moral with aesthetic judgment, albeit the aesthetic
judgment is of moral beauty, Balguy has agreed with Hutcheson that
aesthetic qualities are to be classified as "subjective," in the secondary
quality sense of the word, but has disagreed with him with regard to
moral qualities, which are taken to be "real" qualities of the world found
out by reason, and not "sensible" qualities found out by sense perception
of some kind.

But, as I said, Balguy first stated this as a tentative hypothesis with
regard to the quality of beauty, writing that "I find myself obliged to
suspend [judgment] and to wait for further Evidence."[8] And in a complete volte-face, Balguy appended to the above-quoted caveat the following footnote, in the third edition of *The Foundations of Moral Goodness*:

Since the first Publication of these Papers, I have been convinced that all
Beauty, whether Moral or Natural, is to be reckoned and reputed as a Species
of absolute Truth; as resulting from, or consisting in, the necessary Relations
and unchanging Congruities of Ideas: and, by consequence, that in order to the
Perception of Beauty, no other Power need to be supposed, than what is merely
intellectual. And as to the Diversity of Perceptions above-mentioned, the
natural or accidental Differences of Mens [sic] Understandings seem now to
me sufficient to account for it.[9]

Note well that natural beauty has now been added to moral beauty by
Balguy. And in a subsequent treatise the beauty of art works is added
as well.[10]

Furthermore, Balguy has committed himself to *both* what we would
call moral realism and *aesthetic realism*. And the plausibility of aesthetic
realism (or lack thereof) I shall discuss later on in these proceedings.

But for now let me just review how the comparison between ethical and
aesthetic judgment has worked itself out so far. Hutcheson used the
"subjectivity" of the beautiful (in the secondary quality sense of "subjectivity" as it was understood in the Lockean tradition) to work his passage to
a similar conclusion concerning moral predicates. Thus, for Hutcheson,

---

[7] Balguy, *A Collection of Tracts*, p. 61.   [8] Balguy, *A Collection of Tracts*, pp. 60–1.
[9] Balguy, *A Collection of Tracts*, p. 61n.
[10] Balguy, *Divine Rectitude: or, A Brief Inquiry Concerning the Moral Perfection of the
Deity* in Balguy, *A Collection of Tracts*, pp. 229–30.

the comparison between aesthetic and moral judgments yielded the conclusion that they were on all fours, which is to say, "subjective" in character, in the secondary quality sense.

Balguy's first comparison, on the other hand, yielded the conclusion that the former were subjective, the latter objective, based on the already familiar belief of his times that there is chaotic disagreement over whether one thing or another is beautiful or not but not over whether it is just or right. But in his later comparison, Balguy concluded that judgments of the beautiful and moral judgments were exactly alike in being "objective" through and through: that, in other words, the beautiful and the morally good are both real properties of the world, not the "phantasms" (as Hume would later put it) of consciousness. Thus, in the event, Hutcheson and Balguy ended up agreeing with one another that aesthetic and moral judgments are alike, disagreeing, however, about their basic character.

I want to jump ahead, now, and bring us into the recent and contemporary world of analytic philosophy to see what the comparison between the aesthetic and the ethical has yielded in our own time, bearing in mind that our central question in all of this is why aesthetic disputation exists. I am done for the nonce—but only for the nonce—with what the eighteenth century has to tell us about these matters. It is high time however to bring us up to date.

4

Simple Emotivism

We owe to Aristotle, among many other things philosophical, the distinction between theoretical and practical reasoning. It is the distinction, as many of my readers will know, between reasoning that has, as its conclusion, a proposition about the nature of things (true, one hopes), and reasoning that has as its conclusion an action to be performed that the reasoning will motivate.

Clearly, moral reasoning is, at least in the usual cases, or at least many of the usual cases, a subset of practical reasoning. But there is, of course, practical reasoning whose outcome is action of no moral character whatever, since, for example, I take it to be an instance of practical reasoning to reach the conclusion that we will go to the seashore rather than the mountains this summer for our vacation, and there being no moral imperative either way, hence no reason to call it moral reasoning.

Now there are, to be sure, cases of moral reasoning that do not appear, at least, to have any practical outcome at all in terms of action. If, for example, I try to convince someone that some long-dead historical figure was deeply immoral, present opinion to the contrary notwithstanding, there can be no action appropriate, on his part, to my succeeding in my attempt to convince him of my point of view. Even God cannot change the past.

One might, of course, reply to this that coming to see some historical figure as morally compromised might very well motivate one's present actions in some morally relevant way. For, as the old saying goes, and I presume it has moral import, those who do not know history are doomed to repeat it. And thus coming to see Jefferson or Lincoln in a different moral light from heretofore might well, it could be argued, have implications for present actions.

As a matter of fact, I want to leave entirely open the possibility that *sometimes* one's motive in moral argument is *not* to motivate any kind of action by bringing the "other" to share one's moral judgment but merely to bring the "other" into agreement. (What the significance of this might be I will want to consider later on.) But I also want to emphasize the obvious, namely, that, by and large, through and through, moral discourse is aimed at persuasion for the purpose of motivating action (or refraining to act). When the "pro-life" advocate tries to persuade the pregnant woman contemplating an abortion that abortion is morally wrong, he is not merely trying to get her to recognize, disinterestedly, a moral "fact" (if moral "facts" there be) but to *do* something, which is to say, *not* do something she contemplates doing.

And this brings us to another preliminary matter. In emphasizing now, and in arguments to come, that a, perhaps *the* major goal of moral argument and persuasion is the motivation to action, I am *not* taking any kind of stand on the long-standing dispute between "internalists" and "externalists" as to whether if one recognizes that some action is morally wrong, one is, *ipso facto*, of necessity, motivated (at least to some degree) to refrain from performing it, as the internalist claims and the externalist denies, or if one recognizes that some action is morally right, one is, *ipso facto*, of necessity, motivated (at least to some degree) to perform it, as the internalist claims, and the externalist denies.

The internalist, of course, is not claiming that when you recognize some action to be the morally right action for you to perform, your motivation to perform it will always result in your performing it. All she is claiming is that you will necessarily have *some* motivation to perform it, which may very well be overridden by some stronger motive *not* to. Greed may well win out over benevolence. *Akrasia* is abroad in the world.

The externalist, on the other hand, is not, I take it, denying that very often, perhaps even most of the time, recognizing that some action is the morally right action to perform will provide a motive for performing it. What he, I take it, is saying, is that one *can* recognize that some action is the morally right action to perform without, thereby, having any motivation at all to perform it, just as I can come to recognize that the most convenient way of getting from New York City to Boston is to take the train without thereby acquiring the slightest inclination to go to Boston.

So with these preliminary considerations out of the way we can get down to the business of this chapter, which is to bring us up to date as regards the comparison between aesthetic and moral judgment, initiated, as we saw in the previous chapter, in the eighteenth century. And I will home in on that mid-twentieth-century phenomenon, the offspring of logical positivism known as the emotive theory of ethics, or, in its more recent incarnation, "expressivism."[1]

As we saw in the previous chapter, such a confirmed rationalist in moral theory as John Balguy was inclined, at least at one stage in his thinking, to concede aesthetics to the moral sense theorists. This attitude was still reflected in the recent past in the widespread belief that although the emotive theory of ethics is not a plausible one, its aesthetic counterpart is. Thus E. F. Caritt argued not so very many years ago that

> our moral and aesthetic judgments differ fundamentally in this: It is at least very questionable if, on reflection, we can believe that things have what we call beauty...On the other hand, reflection on our moral judgments more and more convinces me that the relations in which we stand to our fellows are in objective fact grounds of real obligation.[2]

As we have seen in the previous chapter, the eighteenth century knew, as do we, that there is (even though perhaps there ought not to be) "arguing" about taste. That is to say, as neutrally as possible, people do seem to disagree, sometimes violently, about the merit of works of art, and the presence or absence of beauty in nature and artifacts. People do not simply express their preferences and aversions and leave it at that. They try to "defend" them. They try to bring others round to their point of view. This is not the kind of behavior consistent with the premise that *all* we are doing when we call something beautiful, or a good work of art, is expressing a preference. There seems, in fact, to be as much discussion and argument in criticism as in science or politics or morals. This seems to be a "given" in the problem of taste, although as we shall see, in the following chapter, it is not a "given" that, apparently, every one accepts as such.

It seems obvious, therefore, that any theory of aesthetic judgment sophisticated enough to be worthy of notice must somehow leave room for real aesthetic disagreement, or at least bring us to understand what

---

[1] What follows are portions of a previously published paper, suitably revised: Peter Kivy, "A Failure of Aesthetic Emotivism," *Philosophical Studies*, 38 (1980). See also Peter Kivy, "Oh Boy! You Too! Aesthetic Emotivism Reexamined," in *The Philosophy of A. J. Ayer: The Library of Living Philosophers*, vol. 21, ed. L.E. Hahn (La Salle, IL: Open Court, 1992).

[2] E. F. Carritt, "Moral Positivism and Moral Aestheticism," *Philosophy*, 13 (1938), p. 147.

we *really* are doing when we *seem* to be disagreeing. In other words, it must tell us, as, we have seen, the eighteenth century failed to do, *why* we argue over matters of taste. It is the same requirement Charles Stevenson laid down for ethical analysis: "In the first place, we must be able sensibly to *disagree* about whether something is good."[3]

The heroic line would be, I suppose, either to deny that there are disputes over aesthetic and artistic value, a line I shall address briefly in the next chapter, or to dismiss such disputes as pseudo-disputes. There was a time, in the heyday of logical positivism, when the latter move would have been quite familiar, as many disputes were banished in such a way. But it was the result, so to say, of arguing from above. As J. O. Urmson pointed out, the early emotive theory of value emerged from "considerations . . . of a very general epistemological character and did not arise out of a careful and close reflection on the nature of value judgments."[4] And such arguments as there were of that kind carry little weight for us now.

We must turn, therefore, to some less simple-minded form of emotivism than the kind which would see aesthetic value judgments as instances of personal preference expressions, and that alone, if we are to have a hope of finding a successful account of them in that direction and, in particular, an account that can tell us why we enter into disputes over aesthetic value in the first place. The emotive theories of A. J. Ayer and Charles Stevenson provide such models. But, as I shall argue, the accounts of ethical dispute cannot be plausibly translated, in either case, into aesthetic terms. And that is the substance, essentially, of my claim that one attractive feature of ethical emotivism turns out to be of no merit at all of aesthetic emotivism. Thus, in the event, our search for the *raison d'etre* of aesthetic argument and persuasion still remains unfulfilled.

Ayer's emotive theory of ethics was born, as Urmson remarked, not of any profound philosophical interest in ethics but out of a need to defend an epistemological theory against a threat from that direction. And if his

[3] Charles L. Stevenson, "The Emotive Meaning of Ethical Terms," reprinted in *Facts and Values: Studies in Ethical Analysis* (New Haven and London: Yale University Press, 1963), p. 13.

[4] J. O. Urmson, *The Emotive Theory of Ethics* (New York: Oxford University Press, 1969), p. 15.

interest in ethics was ancillary, his interest in aesthetics was even further from the center of his philosophical attention. In his comparison of the two, mention of it only comes in an off-hand way, it being felt, as it had been by Hutcheson, Hume, and the later Balguy, that what applies to ethical judgments "will be found to apply, *mutatis mutandis*, to the case of aesthetic statements as well,"[5] and, apparently, that the latter are in need of no separate examination of their own. This was Ayer's view when *Language, Truth and Logic* first appeared in 1936, and it seems to have remained unchanged ten years later when the book was reissued with a new and extensive preface.

It was Ayer's view that ethical sentences do not express propositions and have, therefore, no factual, descriptive content: "in saying that a certain type of action is right or wrong, I am not making any factual statement, not even a statement about my own state of mind." But there are two things the maker of a moral pronouncement *is* doing: "express-ing certain moral sentiments," and intending to "arouse feeling, and so to stimulate to action."[6] And since no factual claim is made in ethical sentences, no ethical disagreement, properly so called, can exist; for "the man who is ostensibly contradicting me is merely expressing his moral sentiments. So that there is plainly no sense in asking which one of us is in the right. For neither of us is asserting a genuine proposition."[7]

What, then, is going on when two apparently intelligent agents engage in what we all used to call ethical disagreement. There is, Ayer insists, no real disagreement at all; or, rather, no real disagreement about moral *value*; only a disagreement about *facts*, disguised by ethical language. That is how we are supposed to save the appearances of ethical discourse. As Ayer puts his point:

We certainly do engage in disputes which are ordinarily regarded as disputes about questions of value. But, in all such cases, we find, if we consider the matter closely, that the dispute is not really about a question of value. When someone disagrees with us about the moral value of a certain action or type of action, we do admittedly resort to argument in order to win him over to our way of thinking. But we do not attempt to show by our arguments that he has the "wrong" ethical feeling towards a situation whose nature he has correctly

---

[5] A. J. Ayer, *Language Truth and Logic* (New York: Dover Publications, n.d.), p. 103.
[6] Ayer, *Language Truth and Logic*, pp. 107–8.
[7] Ayer, *Language Truth and Logic*, pp. 107–8.

apprehended. What we attempt to show is that he is mistaken about the facts of the case.[8]

It is Ayer's claim, as we have seen, that this view of ethical discourse can be fitted, point for point, to aesthetic discourse. And it is this comparison between the two that we are principally interested in. Ayer writes in this regard, and I quote him almost in full:

Our conclusions about the nature of ethics apply to aesthetics also. Aesthetic terms are used in exactly the same way as ethical terms. Such aesthetic words as "beautiful" and "hideous" are employed, as ethical words are employed, not to make statements of fact, but simply to express certain feelings and evoke a certain response. It follows, as in ethics, that there is no sense in attributing objective validity to aesthetic judgments, and no possibility of arguing about questions of value in aesthetics, but only about questions of fact...[T]he purpose of aesthetic criticism is not so much to give knowledge as to communicate emotion. The critic, by calling attention to certain features of the work under review, and expressing his own feelings about them, endeavours to make us share his attitude towards the work as a whole. The only relevant propositions that he formulates are propositions describing the nature of the work. And these are plain records of fact.[9]

To be noted straightaway is Ayer's contention that both ethical and aesthetic judgments are not *merely* intended, as he put it, "to express certain feelings," but, as well, to "evoke a certain response." What *sort* of response?

Ayer says that the purpose of aesthetic judgment is to "communicate emotion." This communication could be taken to mean the informing the other what emotion you are feeling, that is whether a pro-emotion or a con-emotion. But it seems clear from what follows that what Ayer means by communicating an emotion to the other is getting the other to experience that emotion himself. For when the critic makes an aesthetic judgment of an artwork, according to Ayer, he "endeavours to make us share his attitude towards the work as a whole," in other words, come to feel his emotion, either pro-emotion or con-emotion, towards it.

But the question now arises as to *why* we should want to, have any interest in getting others to share our aesthetic emotions. What's it to us? After all, there is no such compulsion for me to get you to share my positive emotion towards cheeseburgers or Golden Retrievers. It is all the same to me whether you share them with me or not.

Now the *ethical* emotivist has a ready and plausible answer to this question as it regards the expression of ethical approval or disapproval. For, of course, ethical judgments, as I have been arguing, are deeply involved with the incitement to and the prohibition of *actions*, many of which I or those I care about may have a personal stake in. And it is an obvious first step in my getting someone to *do* what I want him to do or *not* do is to get him to share my ethical emotion, my attitude of approval of what I want him to do and to get him to share my ethical emotion, my attitude of disapproval of what I want him not to do. Moral emotions or attitudes are normally motivations to action, whether or not they do in the event motivate, as we have seen. So it seems perfectly plain why there is a motive to persuade in the emotivist's analysis of ethical judgments. I want not only to reveal my ethical attitude in my ethical judgment, but you to *share* it, so that you will be motivated to do or not to do what I desire to be done or not done.

But the problem of course is, for *aesthetic* emotivism, that the explanation for the motive to persuade in ethical judgments will not plausibly serve as an explanation for the motive to persuade in aesthetic judgments. Simply put, there is no reason for me to want *you* to *share* my aesthetic attitude because there is no action of yours relevant to that attitude that I have any stake in motivating. And it looks as if Ayer must have at least been vaguely aware of this anomaly in the comparison between ethical and aesthetic judgments. For it will be noticed that Ayer's theory of aesthetic judgment does indeed parallel the ethical theory closely, as he suggested it would, *with one clear and rather important exception*: there is no reference to *action* in the aesthetic analogue. Indeed, how could there be? Ethical terms, Ayer maintains, are capable of inciting to action by arousing emotions. But in the aesthetic case no such claim is made, the arousing of emotions being there, apparently, an end in itself and not a means of inciting to action, a point I shall return to later on.

Of course one can easily think up unusual cases in which an agent *does* have a personal stake in bringing another agent around to his aesthetic attitude, for motivational purposes. If, for example, I am a museum director who wishes to purchase for my collection a painting that I think sublime, and the billionaire benefactor whose donation is required to make the purchase thinks garish and clumsy (the filthy rich Philistine!), then my strategy clearly must be to bring her round to sharing my positive aesthetic emotion towards the painting, which attitude will then, I hope, motivate her to come up with the cash.

But in the normal, everyday discussions among those who appreciate paintings, and literature, and music, no such motives for aesthetic persuasion are operative. Nor are they necessarily operative in the discussions that critics, musicologists, art historians, or literary scholars engage in. They are constantly trying to bring others around to sharing their aesthetic attitudes. Yet there is no apparent reason *why* they should do so. It begins to seem just a brute fact of life that we do so.

Now Ayer construes "genuine disagreement" very strictly. Two people, on Ayer's view, cannot be truly said to disagree unless they are formally contradicting one another, which, of course, they are not doing when one *expresses* a positive ethical or aesthetic attitude towards something and the other a negative one. Unless one is asserting a genuine proposition and the other is denying it, either directly or by implication, genuine disagreement does not exist. For Ayer, a clash of opposing moral attitudes is not a genuine disagreement. Genuine moral disagreements are disagreements about facts towards which attitudes may be directed or which may direct attitudes. Genuine moral disagreements are disagreements about such facts. And since there are plenty of complicated enough facts to disagree about in a moral argument, there are plenty of moral disagreements properly so called. But although Ayer does not construe clashes in attitudes or emotions as genuine disagreements, he recognizes that we often desire to alter attitudes or emotions of others in order to influence their behavior (if, for example, our behavior seems to be on a collision course with theirs).

Now it does seem obvious that people frequently disagree about facts, and natural for one person to try to convince the other that the other has the facts wrong and he has them right. And Ayer claims, in the quotation above, that genuine aesthetic disagreements, like genuine ethical ones, are disagreements about facts: as he puts it, about "propositions describing the nature of the [art] work. And these are plain matters of fact."

Later on I will have more to say about aesthetic "facts" and about the fact value distinction itself as it plays out in aesthetic and artistic matters. But might we not have here our hoped for reason for disputing about taste? If aesthetic disputes, like ethical ones, are genuine disputes about matters of fact, then there seems to be good reason for one person wanting to bring another around to his aesthetic attitude. He is trying to get the other to get the facts straight, as in all disputes about how the world is.

But, alas, this strategy will not work. For the goal, according to Ayer, in both ethical and aesthetic disputes is for one party to get the other's attitude to change; and getting agreement about the facts is just a means towards getting the other party to share the attitude of the party of the first part. And now we are right back where we started. For it is clear why one party wants to get another party to share his ethical attitude: it is to motivate him to take some appropriate action. But there is no appropriate aesthetic action corresponding to an aesthetic attitude that we have any stake in motivating the other to perform. What is my stake in others sharing my aesthetic attitudes, if attitudes are all that my aesthetic judgments express? How is my life affected if I have a positive attitude towards Bach and a negative attitude towards Rock, and my neighbor's attitudes are vice versa?

Perhaps it might be claimed that the more of my neighbors I get, by persuasion, to have a positive attitude towards Bach and a negative attitude towards Rock, the more opportunity I will be afforded of hearing Bach, and the less of hearing Rock. But surely this is a desperate, totally implausible attempt to save a failing thesis. Who would I have to be disputing with where a negative attitude towards Bach would affect my opportunity to hear Bach. The Culture Czar? Of course there are cases where my opponent's aesthetic attitude might matter to me, as I have suggested above. But for the most part, people who enter into disputes over taste have no effect, one way or the other, on the other: on each other's opportunities to enjoy the works of art they value, or on possible public support for such works.

We are up again, then, against the same conundrum that we have come up against previously, in the writings of the eighteenth-century aestheticians. There *is* disputing about taste, and no apparent reason for doing so. And Ayer's account of ethical and aesthetic judgment, what I have called in the title of this chapter *"simple emotivism,"* cannot provide us with one. But perhaps a more sophisticated emotivism *can.* So I turn now, in the next chapter, to what in my undergraduate days was the gold standard for emotivist value theory, Charles Stevenson's *Ethics and Language.*

5

Do so as Well

Charles Stevenson expounded over the years what he called two "patterns of analysis" for ethical terms. I intend to discuss both of them here, as each provides a possible analysis of aesthetic terms as well.[1]

The first pattern of analysis takes as its "working model" an explication of the proposition "*X* is good." According to Stevenson it has something like the meaning of "I *do* like this, do so as well."[2] In a later formulation it is rendered: "I approve of this, do so as well."[3] The analysis certainly bears affinities to Ayer's. But there are noteworthy differences.

To begin with, Stevenson appears to construe "I *do* like this" and "I approve" descriptively, as I think Hutcheson and his followers would. Unlike Ayer, he takes expressing, it would seem, as describing one's state of mind. Second, the state of mind expressed, which Ayer usually describes as an "emotion" or "feeling," and only infrequently as an "attitude," Stevenson calls most frequently an "attitude," and less frequently an "emotion" or "interest," although he consistently refers to the "emotive meaning" of ethical terms. Urmson has painstakingly sorted out these concepts in his examination of the emotive theory.[4] But as this has no special relevance to my own purposes I shall leave it mentioned and unexplored.

The second pattern of analysis involves what Stevenson calls "persuasive definitions": attempts to redirect attitudes by redefining terms with strong positive or negative valence. The emotive meaning is retained; but

---

[1] This chapter contains further reworked material from my article, "A Failure of Aesthetic Emotivism."

[2] Stevenson, "The Emotive Meaning of Ethical Terms," *Facts and Values*, p. 25.

[3] Charles L. Stevenson, *Ethics and Language* (New Haven: Yale University Press, 1941), p. 26.

[4] Urmson, *The Emotive Theory of Ethics*, pp. 46–8.

the reference of the term is changed, so transferring to the new reference the praise or dispraise which the term carries.

Interestingly (and oddly), it is the notion of persuasive definition that, Stevenson believes, captures the meaning of "beautiful." The second pattern of analysis, he writes, "is conveniently applicable to all of the more specific ethical terms and likewise to 'beautiful.'"[5] The reason behind this lies, I suspect in the word "specific."

There are two distinct ways in which the word "beautiful" is understood in aesthetic and artistic contexts. One way is essentially as an *omnium gatherum* for positive artistic or aesthetic evaluation. In this sense, to call something "beautiful" is to call it aesthetically or artistically excellent. It would be the sense in which any great work of art, for example, calls forth the appellation "beautiful," regardless of its specific features: Grünwald's *Christ on the Cross*, as well as Botticelli's *Venus*, the *Grosse Fuge*, as well as *Eine kleine Nachtmusik*. (Thus the eighteenth century called the fine arts "beaux arts," indicating that their essential feature, at least when they are well-executed, is beauty.) But there is another sense (or use) of "beautiful" when we would want (say) to contrast a pretty face with a beautiful one, a sublime composition with a beautiful one, although "pretty" and "sublime," like "beautiful," are expressive of positive aesthetic and artistic evaluation. (Thus Grünwald's *Christ on the Cross* and Beethoven's *Grosse Fuge* are *both* beautiful and ugly.) It is this specific sense that, I should think, Stevenson had in mind when he suggested that the second pattern of analysis is more appropriate to "beauty" than is the first pattern. Whereas it is, on the other hand, the more general evaluative sense that Ayer is concerned with, I think, in his remarks previously discussed.

If we distinguish between these two ways in which "beautiful" can be understood—the general and the specific—we can present two Stevensonian analyses, one on the first pattern and one on the second, the latter explicitly sanctioned by Stevenson.

For the first sense of "beautiful," I will substitute "aesthetically or artistically good." On the first pattern of analysis, "aesthetically good" or "artistically good" can be understood (approximately) as "I approve, do so as well."

[5] Stevenson, "Persuasive Definitions," *Facts and Values*, p. 53.

The second sense (or use) of "beautiful" suggests, on a Stevensonian account, that there is (or was) some generally agreed upon descriptive content to the term, such that we can distinguish between aesthetically or artistically good things we want to call "beautiful," and those we want to call "pretty" or "sublime," or whatever. In aesthetic or critical discourse we will expect to find this second sense (or use) of "beautiful" coming up in attempts to persuasively define. Suppose Smith insists that Doxie is beautiful, and Dale that she is merely attractive. "Her nose is too long, and her chin too weak for a truly beautiful face," Dale argues. But Smith replies: "*True* beauty is not that bland, blond regularity of the Hollywood goddess; it is a face with character, with expression, with defects—not a face with perfectly symmetrical features; *that's* what *true beauty* is." Here, one wants to say, is the classic persuasive definition as Stevenson envisaged it, revealing a disagreement in attitude towards certain kinds of faces, Smith trying to redirect Dale's attitude by availing himself of the positive emotive valence of "beautiful."

We have, then, to summarize, two analyses of "beautiful," on Stevenson's view. We have, first, the analysis in which "*X* is aesthetically (or artistically) good" can be understood to mean, "I aesthetically (or artistically) approve of *X*, do so as well," "I approve" being construed as a description of the speaker's state of mind, and "do so as well" as the imperative to share the speaker's state of mind. And we have, secondly, the more specific sense of "beautiful," with its more palpable descriptive content, such that we can distinguish among the things we want to call "beautiful" in the sense of "aesthetically or artistically good," those that are "pretty," those that are "sublime," and so forth, and, of course, those that are "beautiful." This second sense of "beautiful" will be involved at times in persuasive definition. At these times, it will, like the general sense, express attitudes, in the form of descriptions of the speaker's pro or anti state of mind.

Stevenson, like Ayer, recognizes that many moral disputes turn out to be factual ones. And thus Ayer's account of moral disagreement is open to Stevenson as well. But Stevenson goes far more deeply than Ayer into the nature of "disagreements" in attitude, vividly pointing up the practical interest that one party may have in the opposing attitude of another. And if such clashes in attitude are not, strictly speaking *disagreements*, on the emotivist's view, they are, nevertheless, of such great practical consequences for us that they invite not only attempts at resolution by laying bare the facts, but by various rhetorical means as well.

It should be noted, in passing, that even though on Ayer's view the expression of attitudes is not the expression of propositions, and on Stevenson's view it is, namely, propositions *describing* the speakers' attitudes, clashes in attitude are not genuine disagreements any more on Stevenson's view than they are on Ayer's. For the propositions expressed, when a speaker says "beautiful" of an object, or "good" of an action, and his opponent says "bad," or "ugly," the former is asserting that she has a certain attitude, and the latter is asserting that he has a different attitude, and there is no formal contradiction: *both* propositions are true and compatible one with another.

Attitudes, then, result in behavior: divergent attitudes in behavior that might clash. Conflicting ethical attitudes are liable to lead to mutually exclusive courses of action: the thwarting of one person's by another's; the substituting of what I like for what you like. Thus the combination of disagreement in facts and disagreement in attitudes accounts for a wide variety of ethical discourse which, on a more generous understanding of "disagreement" than Ayer would be willing to allow, might be described as "disagreement behavior."

It appears then that one of the ways in which the emotivist must explain the existence of ethical disputes and, indeed, the existence of ethical judgments at all is by appealing to the desires of ethical dispu- tants to alter behavior and initiate action. The arousing of emotion or attitude makes no sense as the end of ethical persuasion. It is only plausible as the means to the end of initiating and deflecting actions. Nor, in ethics, would this be an unwelcome conclusion. For we all recognize, internalists and externalists alike, the intimate relation that ethical discourse and persuasion bear to human action: they are both, after all, *practical reason.*

But where is the analogue in aesthetic and critical discourse? What actions could I have need of initiating in calling a painting beautiful or garish? What interests of mine or anyone else's are thwarted if I approve of Bach's music and you do not? Here, clearly, the unexamined assump- tion of direct analogy between ethical and aesthetic discourse breaks down, and Carritt's seemingly commonsensical notion that aesthetic emotivism is more plausible than ethical emotivism becomes highly suspect. For the reference to action, so apparent (and essential) in the discussion of ethics silently vanishes, without a trace or mention, from the discussion of aesthetics.

At this juncture two possible objections might be raised. I am arguing, and have done in preceding chapters, that there is no counterpart in art-critical contexts to the crucial place of action in moral persuasion. But, it might be responded to this, there are, to begin with, the perceptual "actions" of seeing, or reading, or listening to a work of art in a certain way, which the maker of an aesthetic judgment intends to motivate through altering someone's aesthetic attitude or emotion, just as the moralist intends by his judgments or arguments to alter someone's moral emotion or attitude to the end of motivating certain moral actions or discouraging certain immoral ones.

And second, cases readily come to mind, as we have already seen, in which someone might have a direct practical interest in arousing a positive aesthetic or artistic attitude (or a negative one) for the purpose of motivating *physical* actions of various kinds. I might want to change an opera manager's attitude towards Mozart so that he will schedule more of Mozart's operas, being a Mozart worshipper myself. Or I might try, by persuasion, to dissuade some revolutionary from destroying the *Pietà* by trying to convince him or her of its high artistic merits. Many such examples readily come to mind.

As regards the first objection, I have no particular aversion to calling a way of reading, or seeing, or listening an "action" (although there is obvious significance in our being tempted to protect ourselves from misunderstandings with scare quotes). But it is a far cry from this kind of "action" to the kind that conflicts with the interests of others, has victims and beneficiaries: in short, the kind of action that calls for the redirection of conflicting attitudes by use of emotive language. We ordinarily contrast a person of action with a person of contemplation. It is this sense of "action" I have in mind in saying that action does not seem to belong to the realm of artistic and aesthetic discourse, although I have no objection to someone insisting, if he wishes, that contemplation is an "action." A cat can look at a king. It is when she does something else that she may get into trouble.

In any event, even if one were to insist that the goal of aesthetic and artistic persuasion is not merely to change the other's aesthetic or artistic attitude but to get him to perform the "action" of reading the novel you approve of, listening to the symphony you admire, contemplating the natural wonder you wonder at, we would still not have the answer to our question of why anyone should wish to get others to share their aesthetic or artistic attitudes. For there seems to be no more reason why I should care what you read, listen to, or contemplate aesthetically, than what your aesthetic or artistic attitudes may be. I am as indifferent to the aesthetic and artistic "actions" as I am to the attitudes. We are back at square one.

As to the second of these objections, which I have already partially responded to, my response would be that, for the most part, the physical activities envisaged inevitably fall under the head of the prudential or the moral, and the fact that they have to do with works of art, and people's aesthetic or artistic attitudes, fails to make the latter the objects of special "artistic" or "aesthetic" imperatives. It is true that sometimes I may be in a position where manipulating someone's aesthetic or artistic attitude might have indirect practical applications, either in helping to influence their moral attitudes, or their prudential ones, or advance ends of my own. But such cases, as I have remarked before, are bound to be uncommon, and peripheral. Nor have I been convinced by any of the recent suggestions to the effect that there are artistic or aesthetic "obligations," apart from the obvious moral obligations we put ourselves under in our transactions with works of art and aesthetic objects, any more than I think there are any special sexual obligations apart from the obvious moral obligations we put ourselves under by engaging in sexual activity. To destroy a statue is morally wrong (or sometimes, perhaps, morally right!). To try to get the music I like performed more frequently is an act of prudence. But neither moral questions about art and the aesthetic, nor prudential ones can provide for aesthetic discourse and persuasion—except in a remote, tangential way—the counterpart of moral action that makes the emotive theory of ethics at least a prima facie plausible metaethical model in this regard.

Whatever the weaknesses of the emotive theory of ethics, and they are many and well known, it does at least seem to do some kind of justice to the "dynamic" intent of moral discourse. It is at least initially attractive because it can draw a connection between ethical language, motivation, and moral (or immoral) behavior. But it is just this connection that the aesthetic counterpart lacks: the dynamic aspect of ethical discourse seems to find no echo in the aesthetic variety. If what Stevenson called the "quasi-imperative" element of ethical terms is a necessary part of the emotive theory of value, it is a theory ill-suited, on that account, to judgments of aesthetic or artistic value. And to the extent that this quasi-imperative element helps provide an account of ethical disagreement, it leaves aesthetic and art-critical disagreement unexplained. Imperatives are a means, not an end unto themselves in ethical discourse: the end, at least much of the time, is action. In aesthetics that end does not seem to exist; and the aesthetic imperative—the very phrase sounds odd—can have no *raison d'être*. To simply make out aesthetic or artistic value judgments to be expressions of approval with no imperative moment at all severely hampers the capability of the theory to give an adequate account of aesthetic and artistic "disagreement behavior" and "persuasion behavior," which, it would seem, manifestly exist.

At this point the aesthetic emotivists may have to concede that aesthetic and artistic value judgments, unlike ethical ones, lack an imperative force and amount only to expressions of approval. This would mean, as I suggested above, that their account of aesthetic and art-critical discourse behavior would be severely compromised. What will be left will be the ploy that apparent disagreements of aesthetic and artistic value are really only disagreements in aesthetic and artistic "facts." I shall have more to say about this later on in the book. But for the present, I will put it on the back burner.

Perhaps, however, it may be objected here, that in my discussion of Kant, in Chapter 2, I have dismissed too peremptorily what might be called the "social motives" for engaging in disputations over taste, motives that have nothing to do with truth or falsity, but rather with "attitudes." I have argued that although there is an obvious reason why I might want to change someone's moral attitude, from approval to disapproval, or vice versa, there is no obvious reason for my feeling compelled to change your aesthetic attitude, if that is what I thought aesthetic disputes were about. For changing someone's moral attitude will alter their *action*. Whereas except in special cases, there is no aesthetic action I have any wish to motivate or discourage in changing someone's *aesthetic* attitude.

But here, perhaps, are some possible further motives for arguing over matters of taste that, it might be claimed, are compatible with the disputant's belief that our aesthetic judgments are expressions of positive or negative attitudes, not expressions of beliefs about the way the world is. First, we wish to share our positive experiences of artworks with others whom we care about. And, indeed, we might even want to bring others around to our negative attitudes, if we feel that the positive attitudes of others toward works we have negative attitudes toward might diminish their artistic pleasure. Second, we have, perhaps, a deep-seated need to feel a sense of community, if you will, with others, and therefore a need for them to share our attitudes, our aesthetic and artistic attitudes included.

In responding to the first claim, it is important to remember that the subject is *disputing* over taste: disputes about the merits or demerits of works of art. That we may wish to share our positive experiences of artworks with others out of pure benevolence is undoubtedly true. But the sharing presumably requires merely drawing the other's attention to what we have enjoyed in the hope that she will enjoy it too. If she *does*, that ends the episode. There is no dispute, and what has happened is perfectly consistent with the views here expressed.

But suppose she does not enjoy the work; does not evince a positive attitude towards it. Is it reasonable to think *dispute* ensues, motivated merely by benevolence? I do not believe so. If benevolence were the sole motive, my job is done. What motivates me to pursue the question, to present *arguments* to support my case I suggest, as I shall spell out more fully and defend in later chapters, is that it is not, for me, a matter of being disturbed by someone's not sharing my *attitude*, but by not sharing my *belief*: by not sharing my conviction about *how the world is*. Of course sharing one's aesthetic experience is an understandable motive: not, however, an understandable motive for extended, doggedly pursued argument and dispute over taste, which pervade the artworld.

Secondly, I would scarcely deny that we are, indeed, social animals, with a need to feel commonality with others of our species. The question is, what are the ways in which this urge to commonality evinces itself.

Needless to say, shared beliefs about how the world is have high priority. And surely so do shared attitudes, *if* one is an "expressionist" with regard to moral judgments. For one way or another, *moral* values have a high priority for *shared* value. If you are a moral realist, in which case moral judgments are statements about *the way the world is* (and more about moral realism later on), or if you are a moral expressionist, in which case your moral judgments are expressions of attitudes, the connection between morality and *action* assures that we all have a stake in a shared morality.

But what about shared aesthetic values? What is my stake in others sharing my aesthetic attitudes, if attitudes are all that my aesthetic judgments express? How is my life affected if I have a positive attitude towards Bach and a negative attitude towards Rock and my neighbor's attitudes are vice versa?

Perhaps at this point the very general claim might be made that there is some kind of deep-seated, unconscious (?) desire or need in the human species to achieve agreement not merely in belief about the way the world is, but across the board in "states of mind" *tout court*: beliefs, emotions, attitudes, the works. In other words, there is an innate desire or need, in each one of us, whether we are aware of it or not, to have everyone in one's living space be of the same state of mind as oneself, whether it be belief, emotion, attitude, whatever. And the relevant special case, therefore, is that there is an innate desire or need, in each one of us, whether we are aware of it or not, to have everyone in our living space share the same artistic and aesthetic attitudes as us. And it is the latter innate desire or need that drives our disputes over matters of taste, not our interest in convincing another of an artistic or aesthetic truth.

I find the claim, prima facie, very hard to credit. And I would require very convincing empirical evidence to convince me otherwise.

And wait a bit! Whatever happened to *another* human propensity besides that for uniformity? Has my opponent not forgotten *variety*? It is an old saying that "Birds of a feather flock together." Is it not, though, an equally venerable saying that "Variety is the spice of life"? It appears to me one might well claim that our desire for, shall we say, "likemindedness," is only the obverse of the human coin. There is a reverse too, as on every coin. And it is the desire for diversity, which should pull us away from disputes over taste. We are at a standoff. Desire for uniformity is not the overriding desire the critic claims it to be. The desire for diversity has equal claim on *Homo sapiens*, it would seem.

So where exactly are we, at this point in the argument? We have, clearly, failed to find an explanation for why one person feels impelled to convince another person to share his aesthetic and artistic evaluations of works and things. And yet it *seems* that aesthetic and art-critical argument abound.

Quo vadis? Perhaps a heroic move is in order. What is this "seems"?

6

The Aesthetic Shrug

Kant, I think it fair to say, laid the modern philosophical groundwork for the current, widespread belief, taken for granted by most (unless they have a special axe to grind), that there *is* disputing about taste. It seems, indeed, that Kant was going beyond the mere empirical claim that, in fact, people engage in what I have called, to avoid making any commitment yet to its possible content or logical status, "disagreement behavior," or, as I shall sometimes call it, "argument behavior." What I take Kant to have in essence claimed is that when you call something "beautiful" you cannot be doing otherwise, if you understand the language aright, than being a suitor for agreement. But could Kant have been mistaken? Might *De gustibus non disputandum est* be descriptively *true*?

In the previous chapters I have searched in vain for a reason *why* we do as Kant said we do in making judgments of taste. Perhaps now it is time to take the heroic line and argue that the reason we can find no reason why people dispute over taste is that—well—they just *don't*. Or, to put it another way, the reason people do not dispute about taste is that there is no reason to. Kant was just wrong. *De gustibus non disputandum est.*

Now as we have seen, more than one construction can be put on that venerable Latin proverb. It may mean that there is "dispute behavior," "argument behavior," but that there *shouldn't* be. And the "shouldn't" could be construed as meaning that it is pointless to so dispute, for one reason or another, and one, obviously, should not do what is pointless: it is imprudent, a waste of time. Or it could be taken as meaning that it is simply uncouth to question or criticize another's taste: it's not cricket.

On the other hand, one might take the assertion that "There is no disputing about taste" at face value, not as an imperative but as a simple statement of (purported) fact. "It is the case that there is no disputing behavior about taste." Notice: this is not the emotivist's or expressionist's denial that, although there is disputing behavior in matters of taste, there is no disputing about taste, *in fact*, because disputes, properly so called, can only be disputes over the truth for falsity of asserted propositions, and no propositions are being asserted in so-called aesthetic disputes or arguments: emotions or attitudes are being expressed or described. The heroic line is that there really is no disputing behavior in the first place.

But does anyone really ever take the heroic line? It seems to fly in the face of the obvious.

Well here, to begin with, is one example. In a book defending moral realism, a view that I will pay more attention to later on, a recent author, Russ Shafer-Landau, is pressing the point that moral discourse seems clearly to suggest that substantive claims about matters of fact, not mere expressions of attitude, are what is at stake. And, not surprisingly, the point is made by comparing moral with aesthetic disputes. Shafer-Landau writes:

We can well explain the point and persistence of moral disagreement by attributing to agents the presupposition that there is a right answer awaiting discovery. Were they convinced that there was no truth of the matter, most interlocutors would see their continued disagreement as pointless; as pointless as, say, entering an intractable debate about whether red or orange was *really* the most beautiful colour.[1]

Shafer-Landau's observation here is meant as a partial defense of moral realism; and as I say, I shall return to the subject of moral realism later in this inquiry. But what we are concerned with now is merely the contrast being made between moral discourse behavior and what appears to be being offered as an example of aesthetic discourse behavior anent the question of whether red or orange is the most beautiful color, the point being that the moral discourse behavior would be vigorous and protracted, whereas the aesthetic discourse behavior would amount, essentially, to giving a shrug of the shoulders and walking away.

There is, however, a real problem here about what exactly the nature of this contrast is. There is moral dispute behavior but there is not dispute behavior about whether red or orange is the most beautiful color. The problem is this. There is no disputing about whether red or orange is the most beautiful color because, *obviously*, it is a silly question.

---

[1] Russ Shafer-Landau, *Moral Realism: A Defence* (Oxford: Oxford University Press, 2005), p. 23.

But *why* is it a silly question? Is it a silly question because it is an *aesthetic* question of better or worse, and all such aesthetic questions are silly? Or is it a silly question that just happens to be aesthetic?

That it just *happens* to be an aesthetic question there is certainly some reason to doubt. For if Shafer-Landau merely wanted to contrast moral questions with silly questions there are surely many such to choose from, equally or more silly. For example, is the potato chip or popcorn the greatest junk food? But being an *aesthetic* question gives it a kind of clout that a junk food question clearly does not have. After all, aesthetic questions are *important*.

But the aesthetic question Shafer-Landau adduces *is*, indeed a silly question, to be shrugged off and walked away from. It seems clear to me, however, that it is not a silly question *because* it is aesthetic. It is just a silly question. (There are, I dare say, silly moral questions as well.)

The question may be silly, in fact, because it involves some kind of category mistake. For if "red" and "orange" are universals, "the color red" and "the color orange," then the question of which is the most beautiful color seems to imply attributing beauty to the universals. And it does not seem to me to make sense to call *these* universals "beautiful" (although I am not claiming that it never makes sense to call a universal "beautiful").

But it is certainly not a silly question to ask whether a *particular* instance of red is more beautiful than some *particular* instance of orange (in a painting, say) or even whether or not some particular patch of red or orange is the most beautiful color. And it certainly makes sense to ask whether Bach or Beethoven is the greatest composer of the modern era, certainly an *aesthetic* question. Nor is it likely that parties intrigued by this question will give it the aesthetic shrug and walk away.

Perhaps, though, I am making too much of Shafer-Landau's remark which was, after all, made in passing. His point could perhaps have been made equally well, and without the added complication I have been exercised over, by simply contrasting moral discourse with a non-controversial silly question that does not involve the moral/aesthetic contrast (although I will suggest later on that there *is* something crucial about the choice of aesthetic discourse as the comparison class). So I want to move on now to a more out-front contrast between moral dispute behavior and aesthetic or artistic dispute behavior that does, I think, indeed take the heroic line.

In a symposium devoted to dispositional theories of value, Michael Smith is involved in making a contrast between the "phenomenology," if I may so call it, of disputes over moral value and disputes over what he calls "values of other kinds."[2] Not surprisingly, the other kind of value he chooses as an example is aesthetic (or artistic) value.

Smith begins by sketching what he takes to be what I have called the "phenomenology" of moral arguments. Suppose A asserts that some action is worthwhile and B says that same action is not worthwhile. "If the value in question is a moral value," Smith avers, "then we seem immediately to conclude that at least one of A or B is *mistaken. Argument ensues.*"[3] And Smith concludes that this "argument behavior," as I will term it, "seems to me to be partially constitutive of moral value, against values of other kinds."[4]

As I said, it is *aesthetic* or *artistic* value that Smith quite unsurprisingly chooses as his comparison class. He writes:

Suppose A and B disagree over some aesthetic matter: the relative merits of, say, Turner and Pollock. In this case [as opposed to the moral one] we seem much happier to rest content with bafflement at why someone likes what we can't stand; much happier to admit that, since "there's no accounting for taste," so at bottom, we have a *mere* difference in taste.[5]

The most obvious way to construe this contrast of Smith's between moral and aesthetic "disagreement behavior" is a contrast between a disagreement behavior in which *Argument ensues*, that is to say, moral disagreement behavior, and disagreement behavior in which it does not, disagreement behavior in which we give the aesthetic shrug, "rest content with bafflement" and take a walk. In other words, Smith seems to be taking here what I called the "heroic line" and simply denying that there is aesthetic argument behavior at all. *Argument ensues [not]* when the disagreement is an aesthetic or artistic one.

But surely anyone at all involved seriously in the arts will find the heroic line completely off the wall. Argument behavior with regard to the aesthetic and artistic merits of artworks is so abundant, and has been

[2] Michael Smith, "Dispositional Theories of Value," *Proceedings of the Aristotelian Society,* Supplementary Volume, 63 (1989), p. 98.
[3] Smith, "Dispositional Theories of Value," p. 98.
[4] Smith, "Dispositional Theories of Value," p. 98.
[5] Smith, "Dispositional Theories of Value," pp. 98–9.

since time out of mind, that to claim argument does not ensue in aesthetic disagreements, and disagreements over the merits of artworks is to simply to fly in the face of the most palpable fact.

Of course, if one has no particular interest in the arts, or in things aesthetic, then one is likely to give the aesthetic shrug and eschew argument. But that hardly distinguishes aesthetic discourse from other kinds where no one would deny that argument behavior flourishes. If I am not particularly interested in paleontology, I will have no inclination to engage someone in an argument over what caused the extinction of the dinosaurs. It is, needless to say, people who are *interested* in aesthetic matters that display aesthetic argument behavior; and of such there are and have been multitudes.

Now it might be replied that the big difference between moral and aesthetic discourse is that there is *no one* who does not have some stake in moral questions, as opposed to aesthetic discourse and artistic matters, which interest many, but by no means all. However that may be, the fact remains—and it *is* a fact—that among parties interested in aesthetic and artistic matters, argument behavior is just as robust and vigorous as argument behavior in moral discourse, or, for the matter of that, in scientific discourse or political discourse. *Aesthetic argument ensues.*

But perhaps I am putting the wrong spin entirely on what Smith is saying. Here are two alternative interpretations. Neither, though, in the event, will, I fear, end up capturing Smith's intention.

Note well the artists Smith has chosen in his example: Turner and Jackson Pollock. *Both*, it seems fair to say, are great painters: that they have in common. But they are wide apart, radically different, in their particular styles, aesthetic, and historical period.

One obvious reason, then, that if A says Turner is the greater and B that Pollock is, no argument will ensue perhaps because, as far as greatness is concerned, there is nothing to choose between them. Argument will not ensue and the aesthetic shrug will be entirely appropriate.

The problem with this interpretation of Smith's example, however, is that it will not make Smith's point, as I understand it. For Smith is trying to show moral discourse behavior differs from (say) aesthetic discourse behavior in that in the former, argument ensues, while in the latter it does not. But if argument does not ensue, in Smith's example of aesthetic disagreement because of the closeness in artistic merit of the two artists—both of them are great artists—then that does not distinguish aesthetic discourse behavior from moral discourse behavior, since just as there can be instances in aesthetic matters of artistic or aesthetic objects so close in artistic or aesthetic merit that it is impossible to choose between them, there can be instances in moral matters of agents or actions so close in moral merit that it is impossible to choose between them. In the former case we give the aesthetic shrug, in the latter the moral shrug. In *neither* case does argument ensue.

Nor should we be buffaloed by Smith's observation that "Moral differences about the relative importance of justice and self-interest in a particular case, say, seems not to be explicable in terms of a mere difference in taste."[6] Of course, one reason we are not likely to say, when it is too close to call in a moral disagreement, "Well here it is merely a matter of *taste* which alternative you think best," is simply that the word "taste," when used as a conversation stopper to conclude a seemingly intractable dispute, was, long ago, as far back as Quintilian, completely appropriated for aesthetic and artistic discourse, and simply sounds odd out of that context, except in scare quotes, or, of course, with regard to the palate, its *literal* home and origin. But there are, in any case, many idiomatic phrases that serve the purpose in moral discourse. We say, "Well, in this case it's up for grabs," or, "It's a judgment call," or, "You pays your money and you takes your choice," and so on.

Of course if you give the moral shrug when it's too close to call you are not necessarily saying that there is no right answer. You may merely be saying that although there *is* a right answer, we are not now, or perhaps never will be, in a position to know what the right answer is. But be careful here. It begs a very important question in aesthetics and philosophy of art to *assume*, as Smith appears to be doing, that when we give the *aesthetic* shrug in cases where the relative merits of two artists are too close to call, we are, *ipso facto*, in his words, "explain[ing] away the apparent conflict in these judgements by providing a relativistic analysis of them."[7] To say that in deciding whether Turner or Pollock is the greater painter, "It's a matter of taste," you needn't be committed to the view that there is no right answer, no matter of fact here, any more than you are so committed in the similar moral case, where "It's too close to call." After all, there are many who are of the opinion that, in fact, Turner

[6] Smith, "Dispositional Theories of Value," p. 99.
[7] Smith, "Dispositional Theories of Value," p. 99.

is a far greater painter than his academic contemporaries, and Pollock a far greater painter than the one who paints those pictures of girls with big eyes. Why, then, should they not think it is a matter of fact whether or not Turner is a greater painter than Pollock, or vice versa, even though it is a fact unknowable at present, or ever, and, therefore, a matter of "taste"?

In any case, it does not seem plausible to interpret Smith as making the point that in aesthetics, when it is too close to call, no argument ensues. For, as we have seen, that would not distinguish moral disagreement behavior *from* aesthetic disagreement behavior; and to distinguish them would seem to be exactly the point of the exercise.

But another alternative beckons. Remember that although Turner and Pollock are alike in being great painters, they are drastically unlike in the style and aesthetic of their painting and, of course, the historical periods in which they flourished. And so in arguing the artistic and aesthetic merits of the one against the other we may be charged, to trot out that venerable cliché, with "comparing apples to oranges." "Who is the greater painter, Turner or Pollock?" is thus seen as a question occupying the same territory as "Are apples better than oranges?" And as the latter is a question with no intelligible answer, so also, *pari passu*, is the former. No argument ensues, and the aesthetic shrug is altogether appropriate.

Now truth to tell, I have never had the least difficulty in comparing apples with oranges. The reason the question "Are apples better than oranges?" seems unanswerable is that it is an ill-formed question. For what one wants to know, clearly, to make the question intelligible is "A better *what*?" Are apples a better anti-scorbutic than oranges? No. Is this ripe apple better than this rotten orange? Yes. What's the problem?

Well, the objection might be made, the dice have been loaded. Apples and oranges are both fruits. What about: "Is this apple better than that screwdriver?" Well, again, what's the problem? Surely this perfect eating apple is better than that rusty old bent screwdriver, if you are asking whether the apple is a better fruit than the screwdriver is a tool.

But suppose the question is: "Is this perfect eating apple better than that brand new state of the art screwdriver?" Well again, what's the problem? The two objects being compared are so close in merit in their respective kinds that it's too close to call. That is why the question can't be answered. It has nothing to do with any problem in comparing apples to screwdrivers. It is not an "apples and oranges" problem at all but the familiar "too close to call" problem.

There has indeed been some discussion in the aesthetics and philosophy of art literature concerning the question of comparative evaluation in the arts, when the objects of evaluation are widely disparate. My own view is that there is no more problem here than in the comparative evaluation of apples versus oranges. There is general agreement, I think, that evaluation and interpretation of artworks begin with placing the works in some specific form or genre. But I see no particular problem, that being said, in comparatively evaluating the most disparate of artists or artworks.

However, in the event, the question is of no relevance, really, for present concerns, and for the same reason that judging better or worse when it's too close to call has no relevance. For if there are cases of "apples and oranges" in the aesthetic realm that make comparative value judgments undecidable, then there will be such cases in the moral realm as well: cases in which two actions or agents are so disparate that comparing their moral merits or demerits would be, some might say, a case of "apples and oranges," and, therefore, undecidable. Moral argument would not ensue; the moral shrug would. But the point Smith intends to make, in the example of Turner and Pollock, is, to repeat, that moral discourse behavior differs from aesthetic discourse behavior in that in the former argument ensues and in the latter it does not. And if the example really were meant to be one of "apples and oranges," then the point would not be made; for in this respect moral discourse behavior and aesthetic discourse behavior would be on all fours one with the other.

But perhaps there is a further possibility in interpreting Smith's attempt to distinguish between moral and aesthetic discourse behavior, that will yield a real difference. Smith avers that "we are much happier to rest content" with an aesthetic disagreement left unresolved, than with a moral one so left, much happier to let it alone than to argue. And I think that may be true in *extreme* cases. Many have gone to the stake or taken the hemlock over a moral principle. I doubt if there is a case on record of aesthetic martyrdom.

However I doubt this proves very much, except perhaps that when the chips are down, moral issues are more important in our lives than aesthetic ones, or, for that matter, cosmological ones. Galileo, remember, was not willing to defend Copernicanism when confronted with the rack. He gave the cosmological shrug. Argument did not ensue.

At this point I think it becomes clear that we cannot interpret Smith in any other way than as taking the heroic line: in his contrast of ethical with aesthetic disagreement behavior, he is, as I construe him, denying that aesthetic disagreement evinces argument behavior. Argument, in disagreements over taste in art and the aesthetic, does not ensue. And if the heroic line is correct, then it is obvious why we have failed to come up with an explanation for argument behavior in our artistic and aesthetic judgments. There is none; so there is nothing to explain.

But here is, perhaps, another way of presenting the aesthetic shrug, and contrasting it with moral disputation behavior, interestingly enough, not initiated by defenders of moral realism; rather, by confirmed moral non-cognitivists. Their goal is to solve what is known in the trade as the "specification problem," which is to say, the problem of distinguishing *moral* approval and disapproval from other kinds: distinguishing "moral from aesthetic disapproval, for example."[8]

Their initial distinction between moral and aesthetic judgments is entirely consistent with what I have been arguing for here, which is the absence of motivating force to action in the latter. With regard to aesthetic judgments, they say, "Such judgements have different typical grounds [from moral judgments]: they are triggered by the appearance of things; by how they strike us when we contemplate them in some paradigmatically aesthetic way." Whereas, "the grounds of paradigmatic wrongness judgements, by contrast, involve beliefs about the actions and motivational structures of the agent, and their potential to harm others or contravene certain social boundaries."[9]

Where, however, these authors part company with me is in their rush to the apparent conclusion that there is a dearth of aesthetic disputation as a result of how they have put the distinction between moral and aesthetic judgments. They write:

It is not surprising that aesthetic considerations tend to matter less than considerations with strong implications for the expectations that we rely on In cooperation, thus providing less support for social hostility. Moreover,

---

[8] Gunnar Björnsson and Tristram McPherson, "Moral Attitudes for Non-Cognivitists: Solving the Specification Problem," *Mind*, 123 (2014), p. 6.

[9] Björnsson and McPherson, "Moral Attitudes for Non-Cognivitists," p. 19.

since paradigmatic aesthetic judgements are perhaps primarily sustained by phenomenological reactions, whereas paradigmatic wrongness judgements are sustained by beliefs about complex psychological, social, and causal states, they tend to come with less of an appearance-reality distinction than moral judgements do.[10]

There are, I take it, two separate but related points being made here. The first, with which I completely concur—a no-brainer in fact—is that aesthetic considerations matter less to the generality of mankind than do considerations of a moral kind. They matter less in that fewer people care about aesthetic matters than about moral matters, and in that a lot of the time, perhaps most of the time, but not by any means *all* of the time, any given aesthetic or artistic consideration matters less than any given moral consideration. Thus, for example, it seems to me to matter far less that it was wrong for me to cancel an appointment with my friend because the weather finally turned fine, and I wanted to take a swim, than that Michael Haydn and Luigi Cherubini are much greater composers than most concert-goers give them credit for being.

It is the second, related claim, however, that I want to home in on. For it seems to me so profoundly wrong, and the reason all too clear, I conjecture, namely, the unfamiliarity of the authors, and other ethicists, with real, serious aesthetic discourse.

To begin with the obvious, the appearance-reality distinction functions in cases where what really *is* the case is distinguished from what is *not* the case, appearances to the contrary notwithstanding. The Müller-Lyer lines *appear* unequal, but it is really the case that they are not. The sun *appears* to revolve around the earth but *really* it is the earth that moves. And so on.

Thus, a case in which the appearance-reality distinction does not obtain is a case in which parties to a "dispute" give the dismissive shrug: it seems that way to you and the other way to me, and there's an end on it.

Our authors give us no evidence, nor make an argument, that, as they put it, aesthetic judgments "tend to come with less of an appearance-reality distinction than moral judgements do." *Sans* evidence or argument, is this meant to be intuitive?

---

[10]   Björnsson and McPherson, "Moral Attitudes for Non-Cognivitists," p. 20.

Surely it is not the intuition of what I have called above the "art-interested," those who seriously engage in judging and disputing about matters artistic and aesthetic (and I will have more to say about them in a later chapter). Examples abound. It appeared to many that certain notorious paintings were clearly in the unmistakable style of Vermeer until they discovered that they were, in reality, not in the style of Vermeer at all, which now seems obvious even to the unlearned, but in fact forgeries of Van Meergeren. Or consider the D-major Fugue in Book II of the *Well-Tempered Clavier*, which appears so artlessly simple on first hearing, perhaps to the untutored ear, whereas upon scrutiny and repeated hearings it reveals its profoundly complicated contrapuntal artifice. Then there is the seemingly episodic novel, apparently lacking in organic unity, only to be revealed by the literary critic to be closely knit by literary techniques that the casual reader has failed to descry. There are the works of art that appeared great to their contemporaries, and are now all but forgotten except by writers of PhD dissertations, and, of course, those that appeared confused and ill conceived and are now part of the canon. One could go on and on. However it would be to beat a dead horse and belabor an obvious point. The appearance-reality distinction is alive and well in serious art-talk. And to deny it, as an easy path to the aesthetic shrug, just will not withstand critical scrutiny.

In a word, the heroic line just won't wash. The plain fact of the matter is that we *do* argue over matters of taste, and have done (with vigor) since classical antiquity, Aristotle versus Plato being our *fons et origo* for the phenomenon. There *is* robust argument behavior in aesthetic and critical discourse. And we have yet to find, in these pages, an explanation for it.

Perhaps two further observations might be relevant here, in the form of questions. First, *why* are ethicists—or at least some ethicists—so anxious to make out a contrast between moral and aesthetic discourse behavior that makes out the former to be more robust than the latter, or even makes it seem, to take the heroic line, that there is no aesthetic discourse behavior at all, of the argument or persuasion variety? And, second, *is* moral discourse behavior really as consistently and universally robust as these ethicists make it out to be? Does argument so inevitably ensue in moral disagreement, as these ethicists claim?

As to an answer to the first question, we get a clue from statements such as this, by Shafer-Landau, at the beginning of his defense of moral realism, or "cognitivism." He writes: "Only cognitivism straightforwardly pursues ordinary talk of moral truth."[11] And he continues: "Moral talk is shot through with descriptions, attribution, and predication. This makes perfect sense if cognitivism [in ethics] is true."[12]

Thus the argument for moral realism begins with the claim that the phenomenology of moral discourse seems to presuppose it. The most obvious explanation for moral discourse seeming to involve factual claims and vigorous argument in defense of them is that moral properties are real properties of the world: moral facts.

Now of course no defender of moral realism thinks that the argument from the phenomenology of moral discourse is a knock-down argument for moral realism. It is just the beginning: the opening shot; the thin edge of the wedge. But if it *is* the beginning of an argument for moral realism, then it would be, as well, the beginning of an argument for *aesthetic realism*, if it turned out that, in this respect, aesthetic discourse were no different from moral discourse. And if, as I suspect, most moral realists would think aesthetic realism a non-starter, then they would have a high stake in maintaining a stark contrast between moral and aesthetic discourse that would make out moral discourse to be such as to favor moral realism and aesthetic discourse to favor some form of subjectivism, non-cognitivism, or expressionism, to avoid a kind of *reductio*, with aesthetic realism as the absurd consequence of the argument. But as to whether aesthetic realism *is* a non-starter I shall have something to say later on in this inquiry.

Now as to the second question, concerning whether moral discourse really *is* as universally favorable to a realistic interpretation, I will just point out that if moral philosophers looked beyond or even ventured beyond the walls of academia more frequently, and paid more attention to the moral discourse and intuitions of the man on the street, the woman on the Clapham omnibus, or even their own undergraduates, they would find a far more laissez-faire attitude towards moral disagreements than their characterization of moral discourse might suggest. "Judge not lest ye be judged," "Let he who is without sin cast the first stone," "To each his own," "When in Rome do as the Romans," in short moral "relativity," moral tolerance, and the moral shrug may be far more prevalent in the moral discourse of the populous than our moral philosophers of a realistic persuasion seem to allow.

---

[11] Shafer-Landau, *Moral Realism*, p. 23.   [12] Shafer-Landau, *Moral Realism*, p. 24.

But there is, clearly, another avenue yet to be explored. Kant famously characterized beauty as the symbol of morality.[13] And the feeling, or suspicion, or intuition that there is some kind of essential connection between the good and the beautiful, is a recurrent theme in the intellectual history of the West. It behooves us, then, to explore the possibility that it is a *moral* impulse that impels us to bring others around to our aesthetic and artistic attitudes; that motivates aesthetic and critical argument. There may be, in other words, a moral issue at stake behind the issue of whether or not an artwork or other object of aesthetic interest possesses the aesthetic or artistic merit claimed for it. Is bad taste a vice? I explore this possibility next.

---

[13] Kant, *Critique of Aesthetic Judgement*, pp. 221–5 (§59).

7

Immoral Art

It is natural to assume that when people talk about disagreements in taste they are thinking of disagreements in art: in the fine arts as we now construe them. And in this chapter I will direct my attention primarily to those, although taste in other areas of human life will be discussed in a later chapter. So the question pressed here, to put it somewhat crudely, is this. Could bad taste in art be a moral defect, good taste a moral virtue? If so, then we would have an answer to the question of why there are disputes over taste and attempts to persuade others to our taste in art. For, as we have seen, the connection of ethics with motivation to action provides ample explanation for the vigor and robustness and persistence of moral disputation. And if bad taste in art is a vice, good taste a moral virtue, then the same explanation for moral argument will serve for argument over the merits of artworks as well, since the latter are a species of *moral* argument.

But, truly, the question *is* too crude, as put, to answer effectively. So let me endeavor to refine it suitably. To do so I am going to make some very large assumptions about the fine arts, some of which I have argued for elsewhere, none of which I shall argue for here. And to the extent that my reader does not share these assumptions of mine about the fine arts, to that extent he or she may not buy what I have to say about the nature of aesthetic and critical dispute.

Basic to all the rest of my assumptions concerning the fine arts is the assumption of a distinction between the art-relevant properties of artworks that I call their "aesthetic properties, and the rest, of which they are a sub-set. I will not attempt to offer a definition of what I mean by the "aesthetic" properties. Many have tried to do so with no consensus ever having been reached. But I will simply give some examples which I hope will suffice for present purposes. Thus if I describe a symphonic movement as tightly unified, thematically, or a painting as exhibiting a perfect compositional balance, a poem rhythmically jagged rather than smooth, or a narrative baroque in its complexity, I am attributing aesthetic properties to the artworks. Likewise, I am attributing aesthetic properties to artworks if I describe a musical theme as lilting, a painting as vibrant, a poem as harsh-sounding, a prose passage as lofty in tone. These are all structural and what might be termed "phenomenological" properties of artworks. And they can be possessed by artworks even if such artworks lack what I shall call, for want of a better term, "content-properties." And this leads us to another important assumption.

I am assuming that literary works of art, such as novels, poems, and plays sometimes express, either directly or by "suggestion," more often the latter, propositions purporting to convey truths, some of them moral "truths," about us and the world in which we live. This is also true of some of those of the visual arts that are representational, and also true, of course, of many films, and some works of music *with text*.

I am assuming, as well, that works of pure instrumental music, music without title, text, or dramatic setting, in short, what are frequently termed "absolute music," have no propositional or representational content at all. Their art-relevant properties are *all* what I am calling "aesthetic properties."

Works of art with propositional content also, of course, possess aesthetic properties as well. My next assumption, then, is that the propositional content of such works that possess it is, like the aesthetic properties, art-relevant. And so I must now explain what I mean by "art-relevant properties."

The art-relevant properties of a work I take to be those properties of the work that are the ones we appreciate in it qua artwork. They are the properties that are relevant to its merit or demerit as an artwork; the properties we mention as contributing to its merit or demerit as an artwork.

And that leads to a further assumption, namely, that the propositional content of artworks possessing it is art-relevant. Here is how.

As I have argued elsewhere, works of art may express propositions in two ways. Artworks may propose propositions for us to consider the possible truth or falsity of in what I called the gaps and afterlife of the reading, or other modes of artistic experience.[1] By the "gaps" are meant

---

[1] On this, see Peter Kivy, *The Performance of Reading: An Essay in the Philosophy of Literature* (Oxford: Blackwell, 2006), Sections 24–9.

the periods, for example, between the time I put down a novel I am reading to attend to other matters, and the time I pick it up again to read further. And by the "afterlife" is meant the time immediately after I have finished reading or otherwise experiencing a work of literary fiction when it is still fresh in my mind for me to reflect upon.

What I argued for, and will assume here, is that works of art that possess propositional content propose what I called, following William James, live or dead hypotheses for our consideration.[2] A live hypothesis is one that, even though you may not presently believe it, you see as a plausible hypothesis that you might come to believe if you were given convincing evidence in its favor. A dead hypothesis, on the other hand, is a hypothesis that you not only do not presently believe but that you perceive to be totally off the wall, so totally discredited as to be beyond redemption: beyond possible defense. And I argued, further, that the proposing of live hypotheses is an artistic merit of those works of art that propose them, the proposing of dead hypotheses a demerit.

Now one sub-set of the hypotheses an artwork might propose is the sub-set of moral hypotheses: in other words, propositions with moral content. Thus a work of art might project a moral outlook on some human institution, or human agent, or state of affairs. And if the moral outlook is what I have called a live as opposed to a dead hypothesis, then two critics, or two laypersons, for that matter, might reasonably disagree over whether or not that moral outlook, that moral hypothesis, is valid or not, and so, whether a merit or demerit of the artwork. Furthermore, one of the parties to the dispute might well claim that it is a moral defect in the opposing party that he fails to perceive the immorality of the hypothesis the artwork projects.

An example, perhaps, will help nail down the point. One of the most admired, most highly touted, not to say most well-known products of the Hollywood movie industry is the Technicolor epic, *Gone with the Wind*, based on the popular novel by Margaret Mitchell. With its stunning cinematic technique, its narrative sweep, spectacular special effects, and performances by some of the most talented movie actors and actresses of its day, it is on every cinema buffs list of cinema greats, at least of the

---

[2] On this, see William James, "The Will to Believe," in William James, *Essays in Pragmatism*, ed. Alburey Castell (New York: Hafner, 1951).

Hollywood variety. It is of near Wagnerian length, yet thoroughly engrossing. It is a rare movie-goer whose interest flags.

All of that being said, I find *Gone with the Wind* an utterly repellent work of cinematic art, *on moral grounds*. All of its aesthetic merits, which are in abundance, are not enough, for my taste, to weigh the balance of artistic merit in its favor, against its moral defects. It advances an idealized picture of the anti-bellum, slave-supported Southern culture; and its depiction of the African-American slave as a dithering incompetent is morally repulsive. As well, the depiction of the South's "noble" struggle against Northern oppression, during the Civil War, and its "victimization" afterwards by the Yankee "invaders," leaves out, of course, the fact that the South's "noble struggle" was a struggle to preserve one of the most morally depraved institutions in human history, namely the chattel-slavery of a race, an institution which every country in the Western world, except the Confederacy, had decisively abolished. In words to this effect, Grant averred that never had a more despicable cause been fought for with greater heroism. But heroism to advance a morally despicable cause is very hard to admire.

Imagine, now, my being confronted with someone who expresses great enthusiasm for *Gone with the Wind*, and extols it as a cinematic masterpiece. I argue vigorously against her view of the film by pointing out to her the moral defects I have just alluded to above. Why am I arguing?

Here the answer seems altogether obvious. The dispute, from *my* point of view, is a moral one. As I see it, my opponent has, essentially, been taken in by the considerable aesthetic glitz of the film, and has failed to perceive its morally defective stance: the morally bankrupt views it projects. In other words, as I see it, someone who can enjoy and extol the artistic virtues of *Gone with the Wind*, apparently unaware of its moral defects, is herself morally compromised. And it is my purpose, in engaging her in dispute over the artistic merits of the film, to bring her to see its moral defects, and in so doing, bring her around to my moral point of view. My reason, then, in this case, for disputing over taste, is the same reason I would have to engage in any other *moral* dispute. There is, then, no problem, in *this* case, and others like it, as to why I dispute over taste. For the dispute over taste cashes itself out in a moral dispute.

There are, however, a number of possible outcomes and strategies enmeshed here that need to be teased out. The first possible outcome is obvious. I succeed in convincing my opponent of the moral defects in *Gone with the Wind*, she comes to share my low opinion, on these grounds, of the work's merit, and, like me, she can no longer really enjoy it.

But, after all, my view of *Gone with the Wind*'s moral defects is based on my *interpretation* of the work. And my opponent may disagree with my interpretation. So the argument has now become one over what the correct interpretation of *Gone with the Wind* really is: what the makers of the film meant to say. It is an argument over what the work *means*. And that—here yet another assumption—is, on my view, *a matter of fact*. It may be a fact over which parties argue endlessly, without coming to a consensus. But it is a fact, nevertheless, what a work of art asserts, if it is the kind of work that *can* assert. Furthermore, since what a work of art means is a matter of fact about the work, there is no problem as to why we argue about it, since matters of fact seem to be the paradigm instances of just those things human beings argue about and try to convince their adversaries of (a point to which I shall return anon).

A word, however, might be in order here about what I take the "fact" in question to be. I am, with regard to the interpretation of artworks (or any other human utterances, for that matter) an *intentionalist*. That is to say, I believe that in order for an artwork to mean such-and-such the artist must have *intended* it to mean such-and-such. And it is a matter of fact whether or not the artist so intended, as difficult as it may be to determine the intention.

But, it must be added, the artist's intention that his artwork mean such-and-such is not a *sufficient* condition for its meaning such-and-such, only a necessary condition. For the intention to mean, like any other human intention, may go awry, may fail to be realized. And so a further condition, which I and others owe to Paul Grice's account of utterance meaning, is necessary. The artist must not only intend to mean such-and-such: he must choose as his vehicle of expressing such-and-such something that has a reasonable likelihood of conveying his meaning intention to his audience.[3]

Now there are those who have maintained, and those that do now maintain the irrelevance of authorial intent to the meaning of an

[3] Paul Grice, "Meaning," in Paul Grice, *Studies in the Way of Words* (Cambridge, MA, and London: Harvard University Press, 1989), p. 219.

artwork. But there is no need for me to enter that disputed territory here. It only needs pointing out that many, perhaps most of those who discount authorial intent in interpretation nevertheless maintain theories of interpretation which imply that it is a fact of the matter whether or not an artwork means such-and-such, even those who think the meaning of an artwork changes over time, since at any given time, it is a matter of fact what that artwork means. And any theory of interpretation which implies that what an artwork means is a matter of fact, whatever the nature of the fact may be, is consistent with what I am arguing for here.

That having been settled, I want to consider two more possible outcomes of a dispute in which I get my adversary to agree with my interpretation of *Gone with the Wind* as morally defective in the ways outlined above. In the first, my adversary *disagrees* with my overall evaluation of the film. I regard its moral defects as rendering it a bad, unsuccessful work of art. But my adversary thinks its considerable positive *aesthetic* qualities are enough to outweigh the negative moral defects. In this outcome it looks as if our dispute has reduced to a purely aesthetic one. We are agreed on the moral question but disagree on the artistic merit of *Gone with the Wind* because we disagree over its aesthetic merits. If, however, in this outcome, it reduces to a purely aesthetic dispute, we are up against, yet again, our old problem as to why the dispute should persist, which there is every possibility it will. Once the moral dispute is settled between us, what possible stake do I have in getting my opponent to agree with my aesthetic and artistic evaluation of the film? Why care? Who cares?

Imagine, now, a second outcome. Both my adversary and I agree on the moral defects of *Gone with the Wind*, and we agree as well on our artistic evaluation of the work: we agree that its moral defects render it a bad, unsuccessful work of art. But I—and this is the truth—have found its moral defects, ever since I descried them, so offensive that I can no longer enjoy viewing the thing. Whereas my adversary, even though she recognizes, as I do, the moral defects of *Gone with the Wind*, and shares my low estimation of its overall artistic value, *still enjoys it*.

Now at this juncture I am not raising the interesting issue of enjoying bad works of art or not enjoying good ones. It's bad but I like it. It's good but I don't like it. Both have a prima facie oddness about them, and I will explore this issue later on.

What I am concerned with in this place is the issue, specifically, of enjoying *immoral* art. And the question is this. Is it *immoral* to *enjoy* immoral art? Because if it is, then I have a *moral* interest in continuing to engage my adversary in dispute over *Gone with the Wind*, in order to get her to stop enjoying a work she recognizes as having serious moral defects. The dispute has become, once again, a moral dispute, and therefore my reason for carrying on with it is unproblematic.

But *is* there really a moral issue here? Is it really a moral defect in someone who enjoys an immoral artwork knowing full well that it is immoral?

Note that the agent cannot be charged with moral insensitivity or moral ignorance: she *knows* that *Gone with the Wind* has the moral defects above described. Is that really a vice?

If ought implies can, someone who continues to enjoy *Gone with the Wind* in spite of being aware of its moral defects might defend herself from moral censure by responding that one cannot help enjoying what one enjoys, just as one cannot help laughing at a funny racist or anti-Semitic joke, even though one is neither a racist nor an anti-Semite. "I cannot just by an act of will cease to enjoy *Gone with the Wind*," she argues, "any more than, by a sheer act of will, I can cease to believe what I believe; and since ought implies can, I cannot be morally culpable for enjoying it."

The response is not without plausibility. But it is not, on reflection, conclusive. An atheist may *want* to believe in God and an afterlife. He cannot, of course, just by an act of will cease to be an atheist and start believing that there is a God and an afterlife. He can, however, take steps, by an act of will, to seek out evidence and arguments for religious belief, in the hope that such will be convincing enough to defeat his atheism.

In like manner, the agent who recognizes the moral defects in *Gone with the Wind* may hate it that she still enjoys viewing the film. And as the atheist who longs for the consolation of religion cannot have it by directly willing religious belief, so the agent who hates herself for enjoying *Gone with the Wind* despite its moral defects cannot cease in her enjoyment by directly willing to do it. But she can, like the reluctant atheist, take steps, within the power of will, that may lead her to no longer enjoy the forbidden object. She may devote herself to an extended period of moral self-examination. She may read *Uncle Tom's Cabin*, make a study of the ante-bellum South, the "peculiar institution" of chattel slavery, the motives and beliefs of Margaret Mitchell and the makers of the film. And so on. And in the process she may finally find that, like me, she can no longer enjoy *Gone with the Wind*, for all of its cinematic glitz.

Furthermore, this is not a singular case. It is a universal human experience to have desires and enjoyments one does not desire to have, a second-order desire this is called in the literature, because one has come to deem them immoral, or unworthy of a human being.[4]

The question is, to remain with the specific case, is it really *immoral* to enjoy an artwork one has come to believe exhibits deep moral flaws, as in the case of *Gone with the Wind*, knowing full well how morally compromised it is? If the answer is in the affirmative, then it is clear that I have a moral stake in trying to get my adversary to cease enjoying the film, since it is a moral flaw in her character that she continues to enjoy it.

However, I in fact do not know whether or not it is a moral failing to enjoy an immoral artwork. There is, of course, the art-for-art's-sake extremism of Oscar Wilde (if he really meant it), encapsulated in the famous quip from *The Picture of Dorian Gray*, which can, of course, be generalized for all art that possesses possible "moral" content: "There is no such thing as a moral or an immoral book. Books are well or badly written. That is all."[5] If, of course, all propositional and representational content is declared irrelevant to their appreciation and evaluation qua artwork, and a thoroughgoing aesthetic formalism is embraced, then it would seem the question of whether it is a moral failing to enjoy an immoral artwork (or an untruthful one, for that matter) can gain no purchase. There are no moral or immoral artworks. And any moral or immoral content an artwork may *appear* to possess (for it must be in appearance only) it does not possess qua artwork.

I doubt there are many philosophers of art these days who would take the hard line that the moral points of view and hypotheses an artwork may project are irrelevant to our appreciation or evaluation of it, qua artwork. There are *some*. But I am not disposed to dispute with them here. I assume that a work of art is the worse for projecting immoral

---

[4] See, for example, David Lewis, "Dispositional Theories of Value," *Proceedings of the Aristotelian Society*, Supplementary Volume, 63 (1989).

[5] *The Wit and Humor of Oscar Wilde*, ed. Alvin Redman (New York: Dover Publications, 1959), p. 75.

points of view and dead moral hypotheses, as I believe *Gone with the Wind* does. And my question is whether it is a moral defect in the person who continues to enjoy the film after becoming aware of *its* moral defects.

My disappointing answer is that I do not know; I am not certain. My intuition is "Yes." But the only conclusion I am firm in here is that *if* enjoyment of immoral art is itself morally illicit enjoyment, then my attempt to bring someone to cease experiencing such enjoyment is an example of argument over taste that has a ready explanation, which is to say, the same explanation that would be given for engaging in moral persuasion.

At this point, though, I think a more intriguing moral question looms on the horizon. It is the question of whether bad taste is a moral defect when it is bad taste in what I have called "aesthetic qualities." These are the qualities of an artwork that, for the most part, are perceptual properties of its sensual surface, and composition or structure. They have no obvious moral character in themselves. And the question is whether it is a moral defect in character to evince bad taste in these qualities, wherever they appear: in music, in neckties, in household furnishings. To that question, and why it is relevant to this inquiry, I now turn.

8

Is Bad Taste Immoral?

The question before us now is this. Is it a *moral* defect of character to have bad taste in what I shall call here the "pure aesthetic parameters"? And, of course, there is the converse question. Is it a *moral* virtue to have good taste in the pure aesthetic parameters?

Now, as I have said before, I make no attempt to define what I am now calling the pure aesthetic parameters. But it would be well, before we go any further with our question, to remind ourselves what specifically the pure aesthetic parameters are and get as clear as we can, without the aid of a definition, what *kind* of thing they are. So here, in lieu of a definition, are some examples.

If I am enjoying the beauty of a sunset over Buzzard's Bay, on Cape Cod, I am experiencing a pure aesthetic parameter, as I would be as well if I were awestruck by a sublime vista of the Matterhorn. Someone standing transfixed before the shimmering beauty of one of Monet's lily-pad landscapes is experiencing numerous pure aesthetic parameters, as is someone gazing at one of Cezanne's monumental renderings of Mont Sainte-Victoire, or exhilarated by confronting, for the first time, Van Gogh's *Starry Night* (although these works of course possess many non-aesthetic artistic properties as well). Or think of a music-lover blown away by the concluding measures of the B-flat Minor Fugue, from Book II of *Das Wohltemperierte Klavier*, in which Bach, in a feat of mind-boggling contrapuntal virtuosity, combines the fugue subject with itself, and simultaneously with its inversion, which is also combined with itself: all four voices sounding together, either the subject or its inversion. She is, in spades, experiencing a pure aesthetic parameter. So of course, as well, is my friend as he reads aloud to himself the sonorous opening of Milton's Paradise Lost. Nor should we forget those few who experience, with the mathematician, Mark Kac, the Dedekind cut: "the beauty of the concept," he relates, "hit me with a force that sent me into a state of euphoria."[1] After all, if the poet is to be credited, it is the mathematician alone who looks on beauty bare. And just to bring things down to earth, after these flights of ecstasy, consider she who is appalled by the garish tastelessness of her blind date's cravat. That too is the experience of a pure aesthetic parameter, although, to be sure, a *negative* one.

Our question, then, is whether those who appreciate positively the pure aesthetic parameters outlined above get moral points for it; whether their good taste is a moral virtue; and, contrariwise, someone who exhibits appalling bad taste in attire or interior decoration, or the pure aesthetic parameters of the fine arts, gets moral demerits; whether his bad taste is a vice.

But a further distinction must be made. For we really have here at least two different ways in which good taste in the pure aesthetic parameters might be a moral virtue, bad taste a vice: "instrumentally" and "intrinsically." So let me explicate that distinction with an example.

Many past moral philosophers believed that cruelty to animals is not intrinsically immoral, a vice in itself, but derivatively immoral, so to speak, because being cruel to animals, it was claimed, tends to coarsen one's character to the extent that one will, as a consequence, become cruel to human beings, which *is* intrinsically immoral. Thus cruelty to animals is an example of instrumental immorality, cruelty to human beings an example of intrinsic morality, on this view. And, by parity of reasoning, then, kindness to animals is an example of instrumental goodness, kindness to human beings an example of intrinsic goodness.

Applying the same reasoning to the aesthetic case, it might then either be claimed that good taste is instrumentally moral, bad taste instrumentally immoral. Which is to say, it may be claimed that a person with bad taste will, as a causal consequence, tend to possess an immoral character in ways that are agreed upon on all hands to be clearly immoral, and a person with good taste the opposite, namely, tending as a causal consequence of her good taste to be morally virtuous in all of the agreed upon ways. Or, alternatively, it may be claimed that having good taste just is intrinsically moral, a moral virtue, and having bad taste the reverse.

So let's look, first, at the case for good taste's being instrumentally moral, bad taste instrumentally immoral. It appears to be a straightforward

---

[1]   Mark Kac, *Enigmas of Chance: An Autobiography* (New York: Harper and Row, 1985), p. 32.

empirical matter. To establish whether there is a causal connection between having good taste in the pure aesthetic parameters and being a person of good moral character, or vice versa, I suppose one must do surveys: examine people's taste and examine their moral (or immoral) behavior, and do some statistical analysis.

Of course there is going to be a problem in establishing operational definitions of "good taste," "bad taste," "good moral character," "bad moral character," as a prerequisite for doing any kind of empirical research into the taste–morality connection (if any). It is not, for that reason, as straightforward as establishing whether there is a correlation between smoking and lung cancer, for example. We all agree on what an instance of "smoking" is and an instance of "lung cancer." But, needless to say, there is substantial difference of opinion about what constitutes good taste in music or bad taste in neckties, as well as what constitutes a "truly" virtuous character, or a "truly" vicious one.

Actually, though, the problem may not be as intractable as it first may seem. One can envision a variety of tentative examples of good or bad taste in this or that being measured against a variety of tentative but familiar examples of virtuous and vicious character to see if there is a correlation between taste and moral character in these instances. I know of no such research project ever having been undertaken. And that leaves us merely with intuitions and anecdotal evidence. What are your intuitions? What are your "anecdotes"? My own suggest no connection. The notorious Nazi monster, "Hangman" Heydrich, assassinated by the French Resistance, played the violin beautifully and was said to be deeply moved by the music of Schubert. And, as it has been said, the Austrians, incomparable in their musicality, spend a good deal of their time trying to convince the world that Beethoven was Austrian and Hitler German.[2]

But what about the proposal that bad taste is intrinsically immoral: a vice like greed or bigotry? Here, I think, we do not have an empirical question at all. And all we have to go on are intuition, argument, and thought-experiment: the familiar philosophical tools of the trade. So let me test an intuition with some thought-experiments.

---

[2] On the possible relation between music and morality, see Peter Kivy, *Antithetical Arts: On the Ancient Quarrel Between Literature and Music* (Oxford: Clarendon Press, 2009), Chapter 10.

Imagine that I meet a guy at a conference I am attending and strike up a conversation with him at the hotel bar. He appears a nice sort of chap, we discuss mutual interests in philosophy, and I find that, like me, he enjoys telling jokes and knows some good ones I haven't heard. I've made a friend! And I tell him to look me up if he ever finds himself in New York. Sure enough, he does. However, continued acquaintance with him begins to reveal some disturbing traits of character. To not put too fine a point on it, he turns out to be something of a non-violent, but fairly thoroughgoing racist and anti-Semite. Our friendship terminates although he remains, to the end, the same philosophical soul-mate, the same joke-teller, and, in all other respects, an altogether congenial companion and hale-fellow-well-met. A "nice guy"! Our brief friendship has terminated *solely* over my discovery of a deep flaw in his *moral character*.

I want now to contrast this case with another. A close friend of mine is an excellent pianist, as well as a genial companion and general good guy. But there is a deep rift between us. His favorite composer is Chopin (not unusual for a pianist), and I am a worshipper of the God Bach. Worse still, he not only thinks Chopin is a greater composer than Bach, he literally loathes and detests Bach, and can't stand to be within earshot of that composer's music. This wide chasm between us in musical taste, as regards the pure aesthetic parameters, is as wide as the moral chasm would be between me and a racist or anti-Semite. But there is, as well, it appears to me, a crucial difference. For whereas it is unthinkable that I could maintain a friendship with a racist or anti-Semite, it is unthinkable, as well, that I would terminate a friendship with someone *merely* because he loathes and detests Bach and I worship him.

What these thought-experiments *suggest*, not prove, I think, is that the Bach-loather does not, and the racist or anti-Semite *does*, labor under a serious *moral* defect. For the chasm in taste is as wide as the moral chasm (if such things can be measured), but does not have the same effect. I can live with Bach-loathing easily enough, but not with racism or anti-Semitism, even if the racist or anti-Semite poses no threat to *me* and is in other respects a likeable fellow (if that is possible).

Now I am not, I should add, claiming that no moral differences can be endured among friends. Obviously not *all* of the moral stances I disagree with are beyond the pale. And *tolerance* of other people's moral beliefs and attitudes is itself a moral virtue. But, needless to say, my tolerance does not (and should not) extend to racism and anti-Semitism. These I cannot live with.

The point, then, is this. I have tried to construct two thought-experiments exhibiting two disagreements, comparable in *magnitude*, one clearly moral, the other aesthetic. And I have essentially argued that if they are comparable in magnitude, and are both *moral*, then our reaction in each case should be the same. Since I can't maintain a friendship with the racist or anti-Semite, I should not be able to with the Bach-loather either. But it seems clear to me that my behavior in the two cases will be radically different. The Bach-loather I can accommodate. The racist or anti-Semite I cannot. (Bertrand Russell once said that he had thought immortality was a really good idea until he came to realize that it also applied to humbugs and anti-Semites.)

Now perhaps the dissenter from this argument will claim that in choosing the Bach-loather I have failed to choose someone whose aesthetic defect is as great as the racist's or anti-Semite's moral defect. But then I think the burden falls on him to produce a better example (without begging the question). And, by the way, perhaps I can further bolster my point with the following domestic anecdote. My wife is deeply into folk music, blues, and country and western, and I, as I have said, am deeply into Bach (and classical music in general). Yet we have lived in (almost) perfect harmony for many years. One day I asked her whether she would have married me if I were a *Republican*? The answer was emphatic and unequivocal: "Never!" The moral of this cautionary tale being, I suppose, that even where the moral gap is not so wide, and the aesthetic gap very wide indeed, the moral gap possesses a potency to alienate beyond that of the aesthetic.

The conclusion emerging from these considerations, I suggest, is that good taste in the pure aesthetic parameters appears to be neither an instrumental nor an intrinsic moral virtue, bad taste in them neither an instrumental nor an intrinsic vice. But so what, it might be responded. After all, what we are looking for is an explanation of why we dispute over aesthetic taste: an explanation in terms of a *motive*. So perhaps, it might be argued, we are all just hostage to the *mistaken* belief that aesthetic disputes, disputes over the pure aesthetic parameters, are, *au fond*, moral disputes, and that it is this mistaken belief that motivates aesthetic disputes.

The question is, however, *do* we labor under this belief, mistaken or not, in our aesthetic disputes, and *does* that belief motivate our aesthetic dispute behavior? That, again, would seem to be an empirical question. But I know of no research to support the thesis from the behavioral sciences or anywhere else. And as for anecdotal evidence, it is no good to adduce the obvious fact that we do indeed argue over pure aesthetic matters with the same fervor and tenacity that we exhibit when arguing over moral matters. For fervor and tenacity are by no means exclusive to moral argumentation, or aesthetic argumentation. Indeed, the fervor and tenacity of moral argument, as we have seen, is frequently said to be equal to the fervor and tenacity of argument over matters of fact, and in the same spirit, which observation then may serve as the first premise in an argument to support moral realism.

So, yet again, we seem to be at an impasse. The question of why we argue over the pure aesthetic parameters is not answered by reduction of aesthetic disputation to a form of moral disputation. We cannot rely upon the justification for moral disputation to do service for the justification of aesthetic disputation as well.

But another possibility has already been hinted at above. The argument for moral realism frequently begins with the observation that moral disputes *seem*, at least, to be carried on under the assumption that what is at stake in such disputes is *matters of fact*; matters of *moral* fact. And I have pointed out, as well, that some claims to the contrary notwithstanding, aesthetic disputation over the pure aesthetic parameters, as well as other artistic parameters, seems to be engaged in, by those who do engage in it, with the same vigor, the same tenacity as moral disputation. Could this observation be the first premise of an argument for *aesthetic realism*? Does aesthetic realism lie at the heart of the matter? This possibility, and its possible ramifications, are on our agenda. But first I will make another stab at the moral answer to our problem, although perhaps it is something of an attenuated sense of the moral that will be in play.

9

Push-pin and Poetry

Jeremy Bentham famously asserted that push-pin is as good as poetry, push-pin being a trivial game, popular in his day, and said to resemble, by one of my undergraduate professors, the children's game of tiddly-winks.[1] My question is: Is the push-pin player as good as the poetry reader, in a moral sense of "good" to be explained later on. But in order to understand my question, and to answer it, we must first understand Bentham's assertion.

Bentham, many, if not most of my readers will know, was a thorough-going hedonist as well as the first modern utilitarian. As a hedonist, of course, he believed the only intrinsic good to be pleasure and the absence of pain, everything else that is good only instrumentally good, which is to say, productive of pleasure or the absence of pain. And as a utilitarian he, of course, believed that an action is right in so far as it produces more happiness, or less unhappiness than any of the alternative actions open to the agent, happiness being cashed out, as a consequence of his hedonism, in terms of pleasure or the absence of pain. (Only Bentham's hedonism, not his utilitarianism, will be relevant to the present discussion.)

The meaning of Bentham's purposely paradoxical-sounding *bon mot* that push-pin is as good as poetry now becomes clear. If the only measure of goodness in an activity is the amount of pleasure it produces (or pain it reduces or prevents) then push-pin is as good as poetry if it produces as much pleasure. There is nothing further that can be said to make out that poetry is intrinsically better than push-pin, or better than any other trivial pursuit, for that matter, that is productive of the same amount of pleasure (and the same amount, if any, of painful side-effects). I shall call this Bentham's paradox.

---

[1] I do not know the source of Bentham's assertion; but it is well known to all students of philosophy.

To Bentham, Bentham's paradox was no paradox: it was a straight-forward, un- objectionable implication of his hedonism. But to others it might well seem a *reductio ad absurdum* of hedonism. If hedonism implies that push-pin is as good as poetry, then hedonism must be a false doctrine; for, *clearly*, poetry *is* better than push-pin, equal produc-tion of pleasure to the contrary notwithstanding. To plumb this paradox, or *reductio*, if paradox or *reductio* it is, we must first get a handle on what is sometimes called Bentham's "hedonic calculus."

In Chapter IV of *An Introduction to the Principles of Morals and Legislation* (1780), Bentham writes:

To a person considered *by himself*, the value of a pleasure or pain considered *by itself*, will be great or less, according to the following circumstances:

1. Its *intensity*.
2. Its *duration*.
3. Its *certainty* or *uncertainty*.
4. Its *propinquity* or *remoteness*.

And Bentham adds:

But when the value of any pleasure or pain is considered for the purpose of estimating the tendency of any *act* by which it is produced, there are two other circumstances to be taken into account; these are,

5. Its *fecundity*, or the chance it has of being followed by sensations of the *same* kind: that is, pleasure, if it be a pleasure: pain, if it be a pain.
6. Its *purity*, or chance it has of *not* being followed by sensations of the *opposite* kind: that is, pain, if it be a pleasure: pleasure, if it be a pain.[2]

Now what we want of course to see is how Bentham's paradox follows from Bentham's hedonic calculus. But the paradox is merely a special case of the general paradox of equality in value of *any* two things that, pre-systematically, we believe are *not* of equal value, but that the hedonic calculus implies *are*, or, for that matter, are of *unequal* value with the intuitively better actually worse, according to the calculus. So let us put Bentham's paradox in the terms of our enquiry. According to the hedonic calculus, then, Musak is as good as Mozart; or, to employ yet again Hume's example, Ogilby is as good as Milton.

---

[2] A. I. Melden (ed.), *Ethical Theories: A Book of Readings* (New York: Prentice Hall, 1950), p. 264.

Turning now to the specifics of the hedonic calculus, the first two parameters, *intensity* and *duration* require little comment. Assuming *intensity* of pleasure can be quantified—a questionable assumption at best—then it is obvious that what the calculus tells us is that if Musak gives Henry thirty minutes of pleasure at intensity ten and Mozart gives Henrietta thirty minutes of pleasure at intensity ten, then *that* Musak event is as good as *that* Mozart event: full stop.

As for *certainty* or *uncertainty*, the point merely is, one presumes, that the likelihood of Henrietta's getting (say) *n* minutes of pleasure at intensity *i* must be factored into the value of a Mozart event for her, ditto the value of a Musak event for Henry. As well, the time, for example, Henry will have to wait to get *n* intensity of pleasure from *n* minutes of Mozart, must be factored into the value of a Mozart event for him. Will he, perhaps, have to take a course in music appreciation before he can begin to reap any pleasure at all from a Mozart event, whereas Musak pleasure is immediately available?

Furthermore, sticking with Henry for the nonce, we have to factor in the likelihood of his pleasure in Musak being fruitful for leaving other pleasure in its wake, more Musak pleasure or pleasure after the Musak pleasure *in* having had Musak pleasure. And, getting back again to Henrietta, we may consider the *purity* of her Mozart pleasure, the chance of it being followed by the *opposite* of pleasure, say, fatigue from the concentration required for deriving pleasure from such music.

All of these variables must, of course, be factored into the hedonic equation and may help to soften Bentham's paradox by producing the result that even though, at time *t*, Musak produces thirty minutes of pleasure at intensity ten for Henry, and Mozart produces thirty minutes of pleasure at intensity ten for Henrietta, Mozart is *better*. But though the paradox may be softened in individual cases, it still remains intact. For the possibility still remains that even when all the variables are factored into the hedonic equation in some particular case, Musak *will* be as good (or better) than Mozart. And that *seems* the bullet one *must* bite if one is to remain a hedonist.

John Stuart Mill, however, was of the opinion that one could remain a hedonist *without* biting Bentham's bullet. He did so, as some of my readers may know, by introducing another dimension into Bentham's hedonic calculus, namely, what he called the *quality* of a pleasure. "It would be absurd," he insisted, "that, while in estimating all other things quality is considered as well as quantity, the estimation of pleasure should be supposed to depend on quantity alone."[3]

The answer to Bentham's paradox now directly follows. Poetry is better than push-pin because, even though it may give equal intensity of pleasure to the push-pin enthusiast as poetry gives to the aesthete, poetry gives a higher *quality* of pleasure, and that tips the balance. Poetry turns out to be, as intuition tells us, better than push-pin. Furthermore, Mozart turns out, on the same grounds, to be better than Musak, Milton better than Ogilby. Bentham's paradox is thus resolved.

But, needless to say, the nasty question now looms of how to measure the *quality* of pleasure while still remaining within the bounds of hedonism. For if we turn from that philosophical abstraction, "pleasure," to things in the real world the quality of which we measure, what we find is that it seems to cash out in terms of the *quantity* of something *else*. But the higher quality pleasure cannot be higher in quality in virtue of having something else, some *other* ingredient, to a higher degree than the lower quality pleasure, if hedonism is true, because the *ultimate* measure of value just *is* pleasure. There can be no *other* ingredient in pleasure, a greater quantity of which makes one pleasure of equal intensity to another of higher quality, in other words, a *better* pleasure of the same intensity.

But nor can we follow the obvious route of claiming that given two pleasures of equal intensity and duration, the one of higher quality is the one produced by the more worthy activity. For we would, again, be deviating from hedonist doctrine by smuggling in some value other than pleasure that makes one activity more worthy than another, poetry a more worthy activity than push-pin. Yet that seems to be the route Mill has taken. So we have to see how he tries to finesse the strategy.

Mill writes:

If I am asked what I mean by a difference of quality in a pleasure, or what makes one pleasure more valuable than another, merely as a pleasure, except its being greater in amount, there is but one possible answer. Of two pleasures, if there be one to which all who have experience of both give a decided preference, irrespective of any feeling of moral obligation to prefer it, that is the more desirable pleasure.[4]

[3] John Stuart Mill, *Utilitarianism*, ed. Oskar Piest (New York: The Liberal Arts Press, 1957), p. 12.

[4] Mill, *Utilitarianism*, p. 12.

And as to what it means for a pleasure to be "the more desirable pleasure," which, presumably is now synonymous with the pleasure of higher quality, Mill has this to say about the concept of desirability:

The only proof capable of being given that an object is visible is that people see it. . . . In like manner, I apprehend, the sole evidence it is possible to produce that anything is desirable is that people do actually desire it.[5]

The standard objection to Mill's treatment of desirability as measure of quality in pleasures is that the analogy he draws with concepts like visibility is a false analogy. To be a visible thing is to be a thing that can be seen. But to be a desirable thing, in the sense relevant here, which is the evaluative sense of higher quality, is not to be a thing people *can* desire but a thing people *ought to* desire: a thing *worthy* of desire. In a word, "visible" is a descriptive term, "desirable" a normative one. So a value judgment has been illegitimately smuggled in where it should not be if Mill is to be steady to his hedonist text. Or else, the question has simply been begged in favor of the pleasures Mill and his ilk prefer: needless to say, poetic pleasure over push-pin pleasure. Submitting the distinction between higher and lower quality pleasure to *vox populi*, as Mill has done, is fraught with complications that muddy the waters considerably.

Mill, as quoted above, proposes the following test for defining the higher quality of one pleasure over another: "if there be one to which all who have experience of both give a decided preference, . . . that is the more desirable pleasure," which is to say, the pleasure of higher quality. And Mill, clearly, is confident about the outcome of such a trial: when it comes (say) to push-pin versus poetry pleasure, poetry pleasure is going to get the vote.

But how would we really carry out such a trial? And what might be the result?

Are we supposed to ask some group of randomly selected people who have experienced both push-pin pleasure and poetry pleasure which they prefer? Or, to bring it out of the philosophy world and into our world, suppose we randomly select fifty individuals, let us say fifty men, to avoid the complication of possible gender influences, and let them view ten minutes of a professional football game and listen to ten minutes of great

[5] Mill, *Utilitarianism*, p. 44.

poetry read by a distinguished actress. Of those who derive pleasure from both experiences, we ask which pleasure they preferred. By a wide margin, they say "football pleasure." So it turns out that if these results are to be credited, football pleasure is more desirable, therefore of higher quality than great poetry pleasure. For these fifty subjects have satisfied Mill's standard: they have experience of both and opt for what, on Mill's view, is obviously the "inferior" kind of pleasure: the pleasure of lower quality.

Of course Mill does stipulate the preferences of "all" who have experienced both kinds of pleasure is the measure of desirability, which is to say, quality. But how on earth are we to cash out "all"? All the people in Great Britain? In the Western world? The whole planet?

However, putting this imponderable aside, the problem of course is that our subjects have heard the poetry. But have they really had a genuine encounter with it? Only, one has to reply, if they are *qualified* to understand and appreciate poetry. And *that*, of course, is a value judgment. So the normative has yet again raised its ugly head.

So what this little thought-experiment shows, needless to say, is that we must add to Mill's way of measuring quality of pleasure a codicil to the effect that it is the preferences not merely of those who have experienced two kinds of pleasure, but the preferences of those *qualified* to experience both kinds of pleasure, that are to count. Of course the notion of the "competent" or "qualified" appreciator, where the object of appreciation is an artwork, is non-trivial and contentious. I think that Hume, indeed, was perhaps on the right track when, as we saw in the first chapter, he described what he called the "true judge" in matters of taste, whom we might justifiably denominate, as well, the competent or qualified appreciator. In Hume's words, such a personage exhibits "strong sense, united to delicate sentiment, improved by practice, perfected by comparison, and cleared of all prejudice."

Furthermore, as I read Hume's description, it does not imply that the qualified appreciator of artworks be an "expert," necessarily. For the features of the "true judge" that he enumerates can be in the possession of the lay person as well as the expert. They are normal reasoning powers, normal perceptual and emotional sensibility, acquaintance with various examples of the art one favors, and lack of prejudice both in the obvious sense of not approving or disapproving an artist's work because of personal reasons, and being able to appreciate a work historically, which is to say, being able to appreciate the work in its historical context.[6]

In any event, I think I can rely on anyone reading these words as having some kind of intuitive, informal picture of who is and who is not qualified to appreciate and enjoy classical music, or Shakespeare's plays, and so on, just as they can agree that someone who does not know what a touchdown or interception are cannot appreciate and enjoy a football game.

But the first obvious danger here is that those who express a preference for football pleasure over poetry pleasure will be declared, *on that account alone*, to be *unqualified* to appreciate poetry, and their preferences therefore discounted: an obvious begging of the question in favor of poetry by stipulative definition.

Of course no philosopher of any sophistication whatever is going to commit such a sophomoric logical fallacy, a version, some of my readers will know, of what is sometimes called the "Every True Englishman Argument." But to avoid it, it appears to me, one must provide a reasonable account of what constitutes a *competent* or *qualified* "consumer" of any product or activity, be it push-pin or football, or poetry, or painting, or Mozart.... And one must do so, obviously, by means of independent criteria that do not cash out, by definition, in making a "proper" response, which is to say, the choice of what is *already* considered the higher quality pleasure: poetry pleasure over push-pin pleasure, Mozart pleasure over Musak pleasure, and so on. Furthermore, to do that one will have to, on my view, break loose from the shackles of hedonism, by claiming that some human activities are superior to others, on grounds other than, of course, the quantity of pleasure produced. And that, as well, the *quality* of the pleasure is a function of the superiority or inferiority of the pleasure-producing institution or activity.

That is no easy task, perhaps an impossible one. But if it were accomplished, then we might make the following argument to someone who, in the arts, was, so to say, enjoying "push-pin art" more than the worthier thing. "To take more satisfaction in the pleasures that a less worthy work of art produces than in those of a more worthy one is a kind

---

[6] For more on the complications of Hume's "lack of prejudice" criterion, see Peter Kivy, "Remarks on the Varieties of Prejudice in Hume's Essay on Taste," *Journal of Scottish Philosophy*, 9 (2011).

of moral defect (in a broader sense of 'moral' than, perhaps, some might countenance). You would be a better human being, a more worthy human being, someone leading a more, as it were, appropriately human life, if you came to take satisfaction in the pleasures offered by the more worthy, more valuable 'objects' that the world of art has to offer."

And so we have arrived, here, albeit by a rather circuitous route, at a *kind* of moral point to aesthetic discourse. Thus, we may imagine that she who is pleased by Mozart more than by Musak is motivated to convince he, who is of the opposite stripe, that Mozart is *better* than Musak, thereby getting him to be pleased more by Mozart than by Musak, because she thinks she is making a better man of him: a better man, now, in this respect, leading a life more worthy of a *human* life.

Of course, to make this scenario plausible, we must also imagine that the Mozart enthusiast truly believes Mozart *is* superior to Musak: that it is objectively true, a matter of *fact*, that Mozart is superior to Musak. She cannot say, if you get to know Mozart better, get more familiar with Mozart, understand Mozart's music, you will get far more pleasure from his music than you will get from Musak. For that would land her right back in Bentham's paradox: the forced admission that if Musak pleasures as much as Mozart pleasures, it is as good as Mozart.

Here is the situation, then, as it now stands. The proposal is that aesthetic persuasion is motivated by a kind of moral imperative: the wish to improve, in some perhaps distant sense of "moral," the moral character of the one being persuaded. But in order for that motive to be a reasonable one, the persuader must believe that the artwork or kind of artwork being urged upon the object of her persuasive arguments really is a superior artwork or superior kind of artwork. She must be arguing in the belief that the artwork or kind of artwork she is urging the one being persuaded to come to enjoy more than the inferior ones or kinds he now enjoys more do really have the features that make them superior, and that their superiority itself is a "fact" and not merely *her* preference for poetry over push-pin. Her belief may be false; but it must be her belief. In other words, she must be some kind of *aesthetic realist*. Her motive to improve the moral character of her adversary by getting him to enjoy art superior to the art he now enjoys makes no sense otherwise. The moral argument is parasitic on the presumption of aesthetic realism, whether or not aesthetic realism is true.

But now the question arises of whether the moral motive is necessary at all for explaining why we argue over taste. For trying to convince someone of the *facts*—that you have them right and he has them wrong—seems to be sufficient motive *in itself*, in ordinary life, for disputation. Of course we frequently do have some motive beyond convincing someone of the truth for trying to convince him of the truth. And the motive may very well be a moral motive: if he agrees with me on the facts, he will then agree with my moral judgment. But it may well be a "practical" motive as well: if he agrees with me in the facts, then he will turn left on Route 18 to get us to New Brunswick.

In any case, I doubt that most, or even many who engage in aesthetic persuasion have any moral interest at all on their minds, even in the attenuated sense of "moral" operative here. And the point is that belief in some form of aesthetic realism would, absent any further motive, be sufficient motive to explain why we engage in arguing over taste. That avenue will be explored in the chapters to follow.

10

Back to Square One

We began with Hume and Kant. But we are not through with them (or their century) yet, for they still have much to teach us. So, reversing chronological order, let me return first to Kant. Here, then, follow four assertions of Kant's that I have quoted in Chapter 2 and now want to re-examine from a slightly different angle:

(1) "He judges [of beauty] not merely for himself, but for all men, and then speaks of beauty as if it were *a property of things*; he says the thing is beautiful."[1]

(2) "The judgement of taste exacts agreement from every one."[2]

(3) "If we wish to discover whether anything is beautiful or not . . . we refer the representation to the Subject and its feeling of pleasure."[3]

(4) "[He] is not quite satisfied with an Object unless his feeling of delight in it can be shared in communion with others."[4]

Let me begin with proposition (3). I take Kant to be saying here that when I judge an object to be beautiful, the process of judging starts off with my becoming conscious of a particular pleasurable feeling. On the basis of my being conscious of this pleasurable feeling I make the judgment: "That object before me is beautiful." But I am quite well aware, in making that judgment, that the judgment is about *me*, not about the object. For that is what Kant must mean when he writes that in judging something beautiful "we refer the representation to the Subject and its feeling of pleasure." In other words, when I say, "That object before me is beautiful," I am saying something like "That object before

---

[1] Kant, *Critique of Aesthetic Judgement*, p. 52 (§ 7). My italics.
[2] Kant, *Critique of Aesthetic Judgement*, p. 82 (§ 19).
[3] Kant, *Critique of Aesthetic Judgement*, p. 41 (§ 1).
[4] Kant, *Critique of Aesthetic Judgement*, p. 155 (§ 41).

me is pleasuring me in the beautiful mode," or something like that. I am, that is to say, quite conscious that I am making a statement about *me*, and only indirectly about the object.

The judgment of the beautiful, then, is in this respect just the same as the judgment of the agreeable. When I say, "This steak is delicious," I am savoring it on the basis of savoring its flavor, a pleasurable "feeling," and am well aware that I am referring in my judgment to the feeling, not to the steak. So I am saying something like: "This steak is pleasuring me deliciously."

But of course, as we have seen, there is, on Kant's view, an absolutely crucial difference between the judgment of the agreeable and the judgment of the beautiful: we say, "agreeable *to me*," never "beautiful *to me*." And one way of putting that crucial difference is given us in proposition (1), to wit, that in judgments of the beautiful, unlike judgments of the agreeable, we behave *as if* we were making reference to the object, not to ourselves: we speak "of beauty *as if* it were *a property of things*."

Now the "as if" locution can be taken in two ways. I can be correctly described by someone as behaving *as if* a dog approaching me were dangerous, when in fact it is not, but I truly believe that it is. Or, on the other hand, I might be described by someone as behaving *as if* a dog approaching me were dangerous, when in fact I fully believe it is not—if, for example, I am just kidding around, or trying to show a child the safe way to deal with an approaching dog if you don't know whether or not it is dangerous.

Likewise, I might claim that people, in general, behave linguistically *as if* they think beauty is a property of objects, when in fact, so I believe, it is not. In this case people in general, I am saying, behave linguistically, as if they thought beauty were a property of the object, when, in fact, they do so mistakenly believe. I would, then, be espousing the aesthetic version of what is called, in moral philosophy, the "error theory" of moral judgment. (I will return to that theory later on.)

But that cannot be what Kant is saying; for it would be inconsistent with proposition (3), at least as I understand it. For as I understand that proposition, Kant is saying that he who makes a judgment of the beautiful knows full well he is making a judgment about the Subject, that is, himself, not the Object. So he cannot be a victim of the error theory: he does not believe beauty is a property of the object, even though he behaves *as if* he does so believe.

How, then, *are* we to understand proposition (1)? It seems clear that we must understand Kant as describing, in it, the linguistic behavior of someone who does *not* believe that beauty is a property of objects but linguistically behaves *as if* he believes it was. And what kind of behavior would that be? It would be just the behavior described in proposition (2). It would be the linguistic behavior described there as that of someone who "exacts agreement from every one."

But now the question is: What is the party of the first part trying to get the party of the second part to agree about? He cannot be trying to get her to agree with him that the object before them possesses the property of beauty, because he does not believe beauty *is* a property of objects. And what seems abundantly clear, by proposition (4), is that what the party of the first part is trying to get the party of the second part to do is best expressed not by the word "agree" but, rather, by the word "share." Which is to say, the party of the first part is not trying to get the party of the second part to agree to his opinion; rather, to share his feeling. He is trying to get her to be affected in the same way he is by the object before them, namely, to be moved by it, as he is, to the pleasurable feeling that elicits the judgment: "Beautiful."

What I have now finished describing is what I will call Kant's "phenomenology" of the experience of the beautiful. I want now to go on to contrast it with Hume's.

That Kant and Hume come to radically different phenomenologies of the beautiful is of considerable interest, if not, indeed, surprising, since they both begin with the same basic premise. In Kant's words: "The judgement of taste, therefore, is not a cognitive judgement and so not logical, but is aesthetic—which means that it is one whose determining ground *cannot be other than subjective*."[5] And in Hume's: the mind "feels a sentiment of delight or uneasiness, approbation or blame, consequent to the survey [of an object]; and this sentiment determines it to affix the epithet *beautiful* or *deformed*."[6]

Wherein, then, does Hume's phenomenology of the experience of the beautiful differ from Kant's, given their shared first premise? I begin in a seemingly unlikely place.

---

[5] Kant, *Critique of Aesthetic Judgement*, pp. 41–2 (§ 1).
[6] Hume, "The Sceptic," *Essays*, p. 167.

In Section VII, Part II, of *An Enquiry Concerning Human Understand-ing*, Hume is in search of the impression that gives rise to the idea of *necessary connection*. Without delving deeply into this very complex and contentious aspect of Humean doctrine, suffice it to say that, as Hume states the problem:

All events seem entirely loose and separate. One event follows another; but we never can observe any tie between them. They seem *conjoined*, but never *con-nected*. And as we can have no idea of any thing, which never appeared to our outward sense or inward sentiment, the necessary conclusion *seems* to be, that we have no idea of connexion or power at all.[7]

It is basic Humean doctrine that all ideas have their source in impres-sions: are "copies" of them. And if there is no impression, therefore, of necessary causal connection, there can be no idea of it. But, manifestly, we *do* have an idea of necessary connection. Hume's problem, then, is where the impression of necessary connection can be found, since he has already established to his own satisfaction, that it does not come from either external perception or introspection of constant conjunction of events.

Hume's solution to this conundrum, as some of my readers will know, is that the impression of necessary connection is a "feeling" or "senti-ment" that arises from our external or internal perception of constant conjunction: something we subjectively add to it. Having observed one event follow another many times over, "the mind is carried by habit, upon the appearance of one event, to expect its usual attendant, and to believe it will exist."[8] Furthermore, Hume concludes: "This connexion, therefore, which we *feel* in the mind, this customary transition of the imagination from one object to its usual attendant, is the sentiment or impression from which we form the idea of power or necessary connex-ion. Nothing further is the case."[9]

But something further *is* the case. For tucked away in a footnote, not long after the passage just quoted, is the following crucial expansion of Hume's thought: "we experience only the constant experienced conjunc-tion of the events, and as we *feel* a customary connexion between the

---

[7] David Hume, *An Enquiry Concerning Human Understanding*, ed. Eric Steinberg (2nd ed.; Indianapolis and Cambridge: Hackett, 1993), p. 49.

[8] Hume, *An Enquiry Concerning Human Understanding*, p. 50.

[9] Hume, *An Enquiry Concerning Human Understanding*, p. 50.

ideas, we transfer that feeling to the objects; as nothing is more normal than to apply to external bodies every internal sensation which they occasion."[10]

What Hume is claiming, here, is that we tend to project, as it were, our sentiments or feelings onto the objects that occasion them, *as if* they were properties of the objects, and experience them as such. Of course, even if there are such instances as Hume describes, he is greatly overstating the case when he avers that we do this with "every internal sensation." For there are obvious counter-instances. I have no tendency, for example, to "apply" to my kitchen appliances as properties of *them*, the anger they arouse in me when they malfunction. Furthermore, I will be neither defending nor defaming Hume's account of how we acquire the idea of necessary connection. That is not my business here. What *is* my business here, and what I want to argue, is that when one applies Hume's notion, as expressed in the above-quoted footnote, to our experience of beauty, whether or not it is correct, we get exactly the right phenomenology of that experience, for at least some cases, whereas Kant had it exactly wrong.

That Hume thought the notion of projecting our inner feelings, our sentiments, onto the objects that occasion them, as properties of those objects, was applicable to our experience of the beautiful seems abundantly clear.[11] Indeed, one cannot help thinking that the experience of beauty was at least one of the things he had exactly in mind, as a paradigmatic case, when he penned the footnote to that effect. And this interpretation of the footnote is further reinforced by recalling that, in the essay on taste, Hume likened the perception of beauty to the perception of color. As Hume put it: "If, in the sound state of the organ, there be an entire or a considerable uniformity of sentiment among men, we may thence derive an idea of the perfect beauty; in like manner as the appearance of objects in daylight, to the eye of a man in health, is denominated their true and real colour, even while colour is allowed to be merely a phantasm of the senses."[12]

---

[10] Hume, *An Enquiry Concerning Human Understanding*, p. 52n.

[11] For more on this, as it applies to Hume's moral theory, see Remy Debes, "Recasting Scottish Sentimentalism: The Peculiarity of Moral Approval," *Journal of Scottish Philosophy*, 10 (2012); and Jonas Olson, "Projectivism and Error in Hume's Ethics," *Hume Studies*, 37 (2011).

[12] Hume, "Of the Standard of Taste," *Essays*, pp. 238–9.

Thus, as I understand Hume's phenomenology of the experience of the beautiful, it goes something like this. An object excites in the viewer the "sentiment" of beauty, as an object arouses in the viewer the sensation of redness, a "phantasm of the senses," as Hume describes it. This sentiment of beauty, like the sensation of redness, is perceived as a property of the object, as someone once put it with regard to color, as "smeared over the object." In other words, in both cases, we are not aware of a subjective state which we then project onto the object. We are aware of the object as having the property of beauty or redness. We are completely unaware of the process of projection that is going on to bring it about that the object appears to us beautiful or red.

Now because there are, on Hume's view, as we have seen, what he calls two species of common sense, one that beauty *is* a property of objects, that Milton *is* objectively better than Ogilby, the other that it is not, that there is no disputing about taste, it follows that there will be two kinds of perceivers of the beautiful. There will be those who experience beauty as a property of objects and believe it is so. And there will be those who experience beauty as a property of objects but believe that it is not a property of objects, rather a sentiment we project onto objects and perceive *as* a property of them. But the bottom line is that *both* kinds of beauty-perceivers will have the *same* experience: both will have the experience of beauty as smeared over, as "in" the object of perception. A close analogue would be two possible perceivers of the Müller-Lyer illusion, one who knows the lines are equal and one who does not. *Both* will perceive the lines as unequal: change in belief does not result in change in perception of the lines' apparent length. It is a "persistent illusion," as is the perception of beauty "in" the object, according to Hume, if I am correct in my interpretation of him on this point.

Whether or not Hume has the "metaphysics" of beauty right or not, he certainly has the phenomenology right, in many cases. But Kant did not, I do not think. For it seems to me that, at least as I read him, the perceiver of the beautiful is first directly aware of the subjective state he is in, of what Hume would call the sentiment, and on the basis of the feeling calls the object "beautiful." He is not experiencing the feeling as a property of the object. He treats it as a property of the object merely in the sense of behaving, linguistically, in disputation, the same way he would *if* he experienced it as a property of the object, and believed it was. But this, on my view, and in my experience, is simply the wrong way to characterize the phenomenology of our experience of the beautiful, at least in many of the standard cases. So, to repeat, Hume had it right, Kant had it wrong. Perhaps the Kantians will disagree. Well, it's a free country!

It might, however, before I close the door on the eighteenth century, be useful to compare Kant and Hume, in this regard, with another distinguished philosopher of the period, whose stock is currently on the rise, after a long period of eclipse, namely, Thomas Reid. Reid had the behavioral aspect of the judgment of the beautiful right, as did Kant, although in a different way. But whether he had the phenomenology of our experience of the beautiful wrong, like Kant, or right, like Hume, is difficult to make out. It is, however, worth making the effort to find out.

In his *Lectures on the Fine Arts*, Reid states his view on the matter of perception and judgment of the beautiful as follows:

There is undoubtedly a judgement in every operation of taste. In the perception of beauty, for instance, there is not only a sensation of pleasure but a real judgement concerning the excellence of the object. It is the same in poetry, painting, eloquence, and music, &c."[13]

In a later passage the point is reiterated more succinctly. "From what has been said then concerning taste, I hope it appears that it is not a mere feeling, but an operation of the mind in which there is a judgement, and a conviction that there is something in the object calculated to produce that sensation."[14]

The first point to notice, in Reid's position, is that Reid thinks the person who judges an object beautiful genuinely believes he is attributing the property of beauty to the object and that the object really does have that property. He is behaving linguistically *as if* beauty is a property of the object in what I would call the strong sense of "as if." He is behaving linguistically *as if* beauty is a property of the object because he genuinely believes it *is* a property of the object.

Of course Reid recognizes that the belief in beauty as a real property of objects is not a universal belief. If it were, he would not, of course, be finding it necessary to argue for its truth. This is made plain in a remark in Essay VIII of the *Essays on the Intellectual Powers of Man*, "Of Taste,"

---

[13] Thomas Reid, *Lectures on the Fine Arts*, ed. Peter Kivy (The Hague: Martinus Nijhoff, 1973), p. 37.
[14] Reid, *Lectures on the Fine Arts*, p. 47.

where he writes, for example: "Even those who hold beauty to be merely a feeling in the person that perceives it, find themselves under a necessity of expressing themselves as if beauty were solely a property of the object, and not of the percipient."[15]

It is not clear whether this "as if" is like Kant's. I rather think not. Reid is making a grammatical point about our language. And the point is that the grammar of our language is such that we *naturally* speak of beauty as a property of objects. In this, I would say, Kant and Reid are in agreement. But Reid goes on to argue, in I would say a distinctly un-Kantian manner, that the grammar being as it is, is prima facie evidence that beauty *is* in fact a property of objects. So, as he puts the point:

No reason can be given why all mankind should express themselves thus, but that they believe what they say. It is therefore contrary to the universal sense of mankind, expressed by their language, that beauty is not really in the object, but is merely a feeling in the person who is said to perceive it. Philosophers should be very cautious in opposing the common sense of mankind; for, when they do, they rarely miss going wrong.[16]

The conclusion, then, is that, according to Reid, the generality of mankind, when they say something *is* beautiful mean exactly what the grammar of their language suggests they mean: that they are literally predicating the property of beauty to the object. They believe that beauty *is* a property of the object they are calling "beautiful." It is only the rare skeptical philosopher who does *not* believe what he says when he says that the object *is* beautiful.

We are now in a position to see exactly what the difference is, in this regard, between Kant and Reid. Both think that the generality of mankind speak *as if* beauty were a property of objects. But whereas Kant is of the opinion that they do not believe what they say, Reid is of the opinion that they do.

Now, however, we must face the phenomenological question. How does Reid think we experience the beautiful in perception?

At first blush it seems as if Reid is more in Kant's camp than in Hume's. For he writes: "When a beautiful object is before us we may

---

[15] Thomas Reid, *Essays on the Intellectual Powers of Man*, in *The Philosophical Works of Thomas Reid*, ed. William Hamilton (8th ed. Edinburgh: James Thin, 1895), vol. II, p. 492.
[16] Reid, *Essays on the Intellectual Powers of Man*, vol. II, p. 492.

distinguish the agreeable emotion it produces in us, from the quality of the object which causes the emotion."[17]

Thus it would seem as if the experience of beauty in an object, according to Reid, goes something like this. I feel a pleasurable emotion in the contemplation of an object and declare it beautiful on that account, meaning to ascribe to the object the property of beauty that is the cause of the pleasurable emotion. But surely there would, in the scenario so-described, be no reason to think that I perceive the emotion as a property "fused" onto the object, any more than I would perceive my anger at my malfunctioning kitchen appliance in that way. There seems to be no claim of "fusing" or "projecting" the sentiment onto the object, as in Hume's phenomenology.

But perhaps we have been too careless in our reading of Reid here. Note that he says: "we *may* distinguish the agreeable emotion … from the quality of the object which causes the emotion." Yet if we *may* it also seems to follow, one would think, that we *may not*. So perhaps a more charitable interpretation to put on the statement is that in the usual course of affairs the generality of mankind do not separate the quality of the object that causes it, any more than they separate the sensation of redness from the quality that causes it. Rather, they only do so if they are philosophers, or other such, who do so when they are in an analytical frame of mind. One may in thought separate the feeling from the object. However, the normal mode of experiencing beauty is like the normal experience of perceiving color. The sensation is experienced *as* a property of the object.

Furthermore, this interpretation is somewhat reinforced in Reid, as in Hume, by the explicit drawing of an analogy between the quality of beauty and the so-called secondary qualities, although, for Reid, the analogy is not exact. He avers that "though some of the qualities that please a good taste resemble the secondary qualities of body, and therefore may be called occult qualities, as we only feel their effect, and have no knowledge of the cause, but that it is something which is adapted by nature to produce that effect—that is not always the case."[18]

In other words, in the case of secondary qualities, what it is in the object that causes the sensation was thought by Reid (and his

---

[17] Reid, *Essays on the Intellectual Powers of Man*, vol. II, p. 490.
[18] Reid, *Essays on the Intellectual Powers of Man*, vol. II, p. 490.

contemporaries) to be unknown (and essentially unknowable). But in the case of the perception of beauty, *sometimes*, Reid is claiming, we experience the sensation while ignorant of what in the object is the cause, as in the case of secondary qualities, whereas sometimes we know what in the object is causing the sensation of the beautiful, which is never the case with our perception of the secondary qualities. Thus sometimes: "A work of art may appear beautiful to the most ignorant, even to a child. It pleases but he knows not why." On the other hand: "To one who understands it perfectly . . . the beauty is not mysterious; it is perfectly comprehended; and he knows wherein it consists, as well as how it affects him."[19]

It seems, then, given the analogy, qualified though it is, between the perception of beauty and the perception of the secondary qualities, a not unjustified inference that at least in some instances, and perhaps in all, Reid thought the phenomenology of the perception of the beautiful was the same as that of the perception of the secondary qualities, which is to say, we experience the beauty as in the object, the same way as we experience the color as in the object. But an inference it remains, without, so far as I can make out, any explicit endorsement by Reid.

So let us take stock. Kant, it appears to me, has the phenomenology of the perception of beauty wrong. For as I read him his account cannot have us experiencing beauty as a quality in objects, the way we do color, for example. Hume, on the other hand, seems to me to have the phenomenology right, whether or not he has the "metaphysics" right. For on his "fusion" or "projection" account we do perceive the beautiful as if it were a property of objects, even though, on his view, it is not but, rather, a "sentiment" in us which we perceive as in the object.

Reid, in contrast to both Kant and Hume, was what we would now call an "aesthetic realist," which is to say that he believed beauty *is* a property of the objects we call "beautiful" (at least when we are correct in our ascriptions). But the issue at this point is not whether Reid is right about the metaphysics of the beautiful. The issue is whether Reid thought the phenomenology of our perception of the beautiful is like the phenomenology of our perception of secondary qualities. That is, did he think we experience beauty as "in" the object the way we do red or green? And we

---

[19] Reid, *Essays on the Intellectual Powers of Man*, vol. II, pp. 490–1.

must give this question (appropriately enough) a Scotch verdict of neither "guilty" nor "innocent" but "not proven." We can, however, say at least this. It is not inconsistent with Reid's stated position that we *do* experience beauty, at least some of the time, as "in" the objects we declare to be beautiful.

As I have said, I think that Hume had the phenomenology right; and perhaps Reid had it right as well. What I now want to determine is what the intuition concerning this matter is among philosophers and others of the more recent past and of my own time. To that determination I now turn.

11

The Right Phenomenology?

If we have learned anything from the preceding pages about the question at hand it is this. The eighteenth-century philosophers cared deeply about the concept of taste. They recognized that, *De gustibus non disputandum est* to the contrary notwithstanding, we *do* argue over matters of taste, and do so with vigor—indeed, at times, with passion. And they gave considerable thought as to what we are disputing *about*. But *why* we dispute about taste they seemed to have little to say. And what little they did say seemed unconvincing.

But what they—at least *some* of them—had right, as I suggested at the end of the last chapter, was the "phenomenology" of the beautiful, if I may so put it. Thus it seems that both Hume and Reid thought our experience of beauty is as a property of perceived objects, as are colors. Hume and Reid differed as to the ontology of the beautiful, the latter apparently embracing what would nowadays be characterized as "aesthetic realism," the latter a kind of "subjectivism." They agreed, however, that, at least some of the time, we experience beauty as if a property of the objects we perceive to be beautiful objects.

It is of some interest that although aesthetic realism, if that really was what Reid, Balguy, and perhaps Shaftesbury before them espoused, more or less withered on the vine, Hume's "subjective realism," as I shall so call it, had a second life, at the beginning of the twentieth century, in George Santayana's once widely-known book, *The Sense of Beauty* (1899). I call it subjective realism because although its ontology is subjective, its phenomenology is realistic, in that, as the subjective realist would have it, we *perceive* beauty as if it were in the object.

Santayana bases his analysis of the beautiful on what he describes as "the curious but well-known psychological phenomenon, viz., the transformation of an element of sensation into the quality of a thing."[1] It is this "curious but well-known psychological phenomenon" (so-called) that, on Santayana's view, produces the experience of the beautiful, which is one of its special cases. For "Beauty," Santayana concludes, "is an emotional element, a pleasure of ours, which nevertheless we regard as a quality of things."[2] And it is clear, I think, that by "regard" Santayana means not "think of as" but "experience as." Beauty is a pleasure in us that, through the "curious but well-known psychological phenomenon," we perceive as, experience as "a quality of things." Put in another way: "Thus beauty is constituted by the objectification of pleasure. It is pleasure objectified."[3]

Now it ought to be crystal clear to anyone who has read my forgoing account of what I called Hume's subjective realism with regard to beauty that that is precisely the view Santayana has proposed. Santayana's "curious but well-known psychological phenomenon, viz., the transformation of an element of sensation into the quality of a thing" is exactly the phenomenon Hume adduced in the *Enquiry Concerning Human Understanding* to explain the origin of our idea of necessary connection and, as I argued, the Humean phenomenology of the beautiful.

It seems strange that Santayana does not cite Hume in *The Sense of Beauty* as one of the early proponents of the "curious but well-known psychological phenomenon," which he certainly was. Be that as it may, Santayana *does* draw a conclusion from it that Hume, so far as I know, never did. Indeed, he sees it as an explanation for our propensity to dispute about taste. He writes, in this regard: "If we say that other men should see the beauties we see, it is because we think these beauties *are* in the object, like its colour, proportion, or size. Our judgment appears to us merely the perception and discovery of an external existence, of the real excellence that is without."[4]

Santayana counts as holding what we would now call an "error theory" in the matter of beauty, analogous to an ethical "error theory." For he is adamant in his conviction that the generality of mankind is *mistaken* in its belief that "these beauties *are* in the object, like its colour, proportions,

---

[1] George Santayana, *The Sense of Beauty: Being the Outline of Aesthetic Theory* (New York: Random House, 1955), p. 47.

[2] Santayana, *The Sense of Beauty*, p. 50.   [3] Santayana, *The Sense of Beauty*, p. 54.

[4] Santayana, *The Sense of Beauty*, p. 47.

or size." For Santayana insists, obviously adhering to the venerable distinction between fact and value:

But this is radically absurd and contradictory. Beauty, as we have seen, is a value; it cannot be conceived as an independent existence which affects our senses and which we consequently perceive. It exists in perception, and cannot exist otherwise. A beauty not perceived is a pleasure not felt; and a contradiction.[5]

But the crucial point for our purposes is that Santayana has provided a believable explanation for our propensity to argue over matters of taste. It is because we are, in general, whether mistaken or not, dyed-in-the-wool aesthetic realists. We think beauty is a real property of objects and that when we disagree about matters of the beautiful we are disagreeing about matters of fact.

Now there is, I imagine, a myriad of particular, personal reasons one might have for initiating and pursuing an argument. But let me propose that there are two major, basic, ubiquitous reasons for doing so, if one is arguing in good faith: that is, if one is arguing not simply "for the sake of arguing," because one likes to argue, or one likes to annoy people, or whatever, but because one has a genuine, shall we say "rational" stake in the argument. One argues, generally, with the ultimate aim of motivating one's opponent to some specific action, or convincing one's opponent that one's belief is true and his is not. Let me try to clarify that.

One thing, as we have seen, that makes ethical emotivism more plausible than aesthetic emotivism is that the ethical emotivist can make sense of ethical disputation whereas the aesthetic emotivist cannot make sense of aesthetic disputation. For the conclusion of "practical reasoning" is *action*. And if I want to convince you to act in a certain way then perhaps I can do so by bringing you to morally approve of the action, moral approval being, on the emotivists view, an emotion that *may* in the event motivate one to perform the action in question, although, of course, the motivation may not, after all, be strong enough to overcome a motive or motives pulling in the opposite direction.

However, as I have argued above, there normally seems to be no action the partaker in an aesthetic dispute would have a stake in motivating, so no reason to bring an opponent around to her attitude of aesthetic approval or disapproval. And thus the aesthetic emotivist has no

---

[5] Santayana, *The Sense of Beauty*, p. 47.

explanation for why we engage in aesthetic disputes, which manifestly we do. Furthermore, it then appears that one of the two common reasons for engaging in dispute, namely to motivate to action, usually cannot be a reason to engage in aesthetic disputation, since there is no relevant action, normally, at issue.

That leaves us with the second motive for engaging in dispute, in a word, *the truth*. It is, I suggest, a completely adequate explanation for why one is arguing with an adversary that one thinks *he* has the facts right and his adversary has them wrong. And that, of course, is exactly what Santayana was assuming when he averred that "If we say that other men should see the beauties we see, it is because we think these beauties *are* in the object." In other words, our objective in aesthetic dispute is solely convincing someone of *the truth*.

Now of course this is not to deny that often, perhaps even most of the time, our attempts to get others to perceive our truths is instrumental: is, in other words, to get them to perform actions we desire them to perform, and that we have reason to believe they will perform if they come to share our beliefs. What I *am* urging is that such ulterior motives, though they are frequently *sufficient* to motivate dispute, are not *necessary*. It is, as well, *sufficient* reason to engage in dispute that one believes one is in possession of the truth and the other is not. That, it seems to me, has ample support in the phenomenology of human "disputation behavior."

When I claim, however, that the desire to convince another of the truth of one's belief about how the world is is completely sufficient justification, no further explanation required, for entering into a dispute, that claim requires some qualification. For, obviously, there are matters of truth and falsity that are fruitless and silly to think about, let alone dispute over. It is hard to imagine (but not impossible), for example, entering into a dispute over how many termites there are on Cape Cod, and think that such a dispute can be explained on the grounds that it is a question of truth about the way the world is, no further explanation required, full stop.

Well yes: I presume there is a background condition on all disputes over the truth and falsity of beliefs that make sense. The condition is, simply put, and I put it vaguely with purposeful intent, the question be of *interest*, at least to the parties of the dispute, and that even though *I* might not find it of interest, I can, in spite of that, conceive or imagine how it could be of interest to two sane human beings disputing the question.

So qualified, then, the claim is that if a dispute satisfies what might be called the "interest condition," then it is a sufficient explanation for engaging in it, that it concerns a certain belief about the way the world is, no further explanation required. Furthermore, although what makes a question of the way the world is interesting may frequently be its implications for action, or its consequences, one way or the other, that is not by any means *always* the case. And when it is not, the motive for disputing is finding out the truth, pure and simple, no questions asked, full stop. This is the case, for example, with questions in cosmology or paleontology, and the case most of the time in history. And so I am suggesting, and will be arguing in what comes, it is the case most of the time in disputes over taste.

Here, then, is the point at which we now are. I have claimed that Hume and Reid, and now Santayana, had the phenomenology of the beautiful right in this respect. They all were claiming that we experience the beautiful not as a feeling or sensation in us, although for Hume and Santayana that is its source, but as a quality *in* the object we denominate "beautiful": "smeared" over it like red over a tomato. That claim, although I am not totally withdrawing it, requires considerable qualification and amplification if it is going to withstand scrutiny.

Furthermore, following Santayana here, if I read him correctly, I will be arguing that the correct explanation for the wide-spread, long-standing existence of disputation over taste, in the West, from antiquity to the present, is the background experience of aesthetic realism: that is, the experience of aesthetic properties as "in" the objects we describe in aesthetic terms. And the serious exploration of this claim will occupy me in the rest of this book.

Let me begin with the phenomenology. The idea that we perceive beauty as a property of objects, like their color, seems most plausible when one is thinking of relatively simple objects: a flower, for example, or the face of Botticelli's *Venus*. But when one ascribes beauty to an entire symphony or a Gothic cathedral, the experience, obviously, seems to be of a far more complicated kind; and locating the beauty "in" the object, as the redness in the rose, begins to seem far from obvious.

As well, as we have seen, the term "beautiful" itself has had, at least since the eighteenth century, two more or less distinct uses. On the one hand, in what we might call its "general evaluative use," the term "beautiful" connotes the success, the high quality of a work of art. It is surely this general, evaluative sense of the term that, for example, Hume was employing in the essay on taste. And on this use of the word, for example, the *Iliad* and the *Aeneid* are both "beautiful."

On the other hand, already in the eighteenth century, the term "beautiful" had taken on another usage as well, shall we say, a more "descriptive" usage, exemplified, most prominently, in the widely recognized distinction between the "beautiful" and the "sublime." Thus, on this use of the term "beautiful," both the *Iliad* and the *Aeneid*, two favorite eighteenth-century examples, would be admirable works of art. However, the *Iliad* would not be termed "beautiful" but "sublime," and the *Aeneid* not "sublime" but "beautiful."

I shall call this descriptive use of the term "beautiful" its "aesthetic" use, because, when used in this way, the "beautiful" joins the large company of what Frank Sibley famously demarcated and described as "aesthetic concepts," such as "graceful," "delicate," "balanced," "tightly knit," and so on, and so on.[6] And in what follows I shall be using the term "beautiful" exclusively in its aesthetic sense.

But we will now need a term or terms to substitute for the evaluative sense of "beautiful," which I have here eschewed. And since I will be dealing here almost exclusively with our disputes concerning taste in art, the terms I will adopt for the evaluative sense or use of the term "beautiful," of which there are many, will be such as "great work of art," "good work of art," "successful work of art," "poor work of art," and so forth. (There are, needless to say, numerous phrases in the English language to praise or dispraise works of art.)

But there is more terminological business yet to come. It concerns the much debated term "aesthetic."

The term "aesthetic" has come to be used to refer to all of the aspects and properties of works of art that are relevant to their appreciation, description, and evaluation *as works of art*, qua artworks, although this usage does not, of course, rule out the possibility of other things besides artworks being appreciated, described, and evaluated aesthetically. But increasingly, philosophers of art have wanted to distinguish between

---

[6] Frank Sibley, "Aesthetic Concepts," *Philosophical Review*, 68 (1959).

"aesthetic" properties of artworks and *other* of their art-relevant properties, reserving the term "aesthetic" for what might be thought of as their
"phenomenological" or "structural" properties, the properties that can be
described in "aesthetic" terms: beauty, gracefulness, and the rest. And
I intend to acquiesce in this distinction myself, as I have done in the past.

Thus I will call such properties of an artwork as the thesis or theses
that a novelist may have expressed in her novel for our consideration as
non-aesthetic art-relevant properties of the artwork, and I will call such
properties of an artwork as the "lilting" quality of the second theme in
the first movement of Mozart's Jupiter Symphony as an aesthetic art-
relevant property of an artwork.

And with these distinctions and qualifications to hand we can now see
how simplistic (but not mistaken) it was to say that Hume had the
phenomenology of beauty right. For we must now see that "beauty," as
I am using that term, is just one among many aesthetic properties an
artwork might possess, as I am using the term "aesthetic." Furthermore,
we must now see that many works of art have far more art-relevant
properties than their aesthetic ones and, as we now see, far more
aesthetic ones than beauty, in its aesthetic use. So when we ask the
question, Why do we dispute over taste? we must consider that if there
is a dispute about taste, it may be a dispute about an artwork's non-
aesthetic art-relevant properties, or about its aesthetic art-relevant properties, or about both. Furthermore, the dispute may be, as well, over the
value of an artwork: whether it is a great work of art, or a poor one, or
something in between.

And given all of that, it now seems that yet another point of terminology is in the offing. I shall call a dispute over the non-aesthetic art-
relevant properties of an artwork a dispute over "interpretation." I shall
call a dispute over the aesthetic art-relevant properties of an artwork a
dispute over "analysis." And, finally, I shall call a dispute over an
artwork's merit or demerit, not surprisingly, a dispute over "artistic
evaluation."

Here, now, is where we stand. I have suggested that there are two basic
and pervasive reasons why, normally, people become embroiled in
disputes: to motivate their adversaries to action, or to convince them of
the truth, no other ulterior motive required for the latter. Furthermore,
I have argued in preceding chapters that motivation to action does not
constitute a convincing reason for disputes over taste, because there does

not usually seem to be any relevant action in the offing for the disputants to motivate one way or the other. So that leaves the second alternative; and that alternative I intend to explore in the remaining chapters.

What I am suggesting, then, is that it is arguing to the best explanation to argue that the basic, most pervasive reason one enthusiast normally disputes with another over a matter of taste is that the party of the first part thinks her taste-judgment is expressing a *truth* about the world of which she desires to convince the party of the second part. The party of the first part is, in other words, a "realist" with regard to the art relevant properties of artworks: an "art-realist," as I will call such a person. Furthermore, she is an aesthetic realist with regard to the aesthetic properties of artworks and is, shall we say, a value realist with regard to the relative value of artworks.

We therefore have a far more complicated picture to puzzle out than is suggested by the simple description "aesthetic realism." Russ Shafer-Landau, a recent defender of what is known in the trade as "moral realism," has described it in the following way. "Realists [in moral theory] see moral judgements as beliefs, some of which are true, and true in virtue of correctly reporting moral facts."[7]

Following Shafer-Landau (who will be heard from again later on), I will say that those who dispute about taste, do so because they (explicitly or implicitly) believe one, or two, or all of the following, depending upon what specifically the dispute is about. They see judgments concerning non-aesthetic art-relevant properties of artworks as expressing beliefs, some of which are true, and true in virtue of correctly reporting non-aesthetic art-relevant facts. They see judgments concerning aesthetic art-relevant properties of artworks as expressing beliefs, some of which are true, and true in virtue of correctly reporting aesthetic art-relevant facts. And they see judgments concerning the relative value of artworks as expressing beliefs, some of which are true, and true in virtue of correctly reporting art value facts. That they see taste judgments in this way, whether or not they are correct in so seeing them, explains *why* they engage in disputes over taste. They are, in effect, "art realists." And what they think is "real" about art they try to convince others of, no further motive required to make their behavior intelligible.

---

[7] Shafer-Landau, *Moral Realism*, p. 17.

It remains now for us to, in the succeeding chapters, examine each of these kinds of dispute over taste, the disputes concerning non-aesthetic art-relevant properties, the disputes concerning aesthetic art-relevant properties, and the disputes concerning relative artistic merit, and decide whether, first, it makes sense to explain them as motivated by the disputants' explicit or implicit assumption of artistic realism, and, second, whether the assumption of artistic realism is warranted, in all, or any of its forms.

12

The Truth of Interpretation

In posing the question of why we dispute over taste I of course assumed that we *do* dispute over taste. But who *are* these "we"?

In this, and the following chapters, I will, as I have said, explore the three kinds of disputing over taste that I have distinguished, namely, disputes over interpretation, disputes over analysis, and disputes over evaluation of artworks, with the hypothesis on the table that those who engage in such disputes normally do so not to motivate their opponents to action but to convince them of the truth which they believe is in their possession and not in their opponents'. But, to repeat the question with which I began this chapter, Who *are* the "we" who do the disputing?

In claiming that "we" *do* dispute over taste, I am not, of course, claiming that *everyone* does. Many folks, not just shallow pates but highly intelligent citizens, do not have the least interest in any of the arts and, therefore, do not engage in disputes over them. So the first, altogether obvious and uncontroversial stipulation of the "we" who dispute over taste is, the "we" who are interested enough in and acquainted enough with one or more of the arts to have opinions about artworks they wish to defend and convince others of.

Of course the "we" so stipulated is a very large, amorphous group. And the range of acquaintance with and expertise in the arts will vary from the slight to the very great. So my next step, therefore, is this. I emphatically do *not* want to limit the "we" to those at the upper end of the range. I include in the "we" who dispute over taste the professors of English literature, musicologists, art historians, and other learned worthies, but, as well the man on the street, the woman on the Clapham omnibus, and all of those in between.

Whom, then, do I exclude? In a word, those with an axe to grind, which is to say, those with a "theory" that precludes disputation over taste, one way or another, as fruitless or impossible. And I put "theory" in scare quotes because I do not only want to include under that rubric academic pundits with sophisticated theses to the effect that *De gustibus non disputandum est*, but ordinary citizens who think, for one informal reason or another, that *De gustibus non disputandum est* is just plain common sense, a "species" of common sense, as Hume put it in the essay on taste, to which some lay persons may subscribe.

The "we," then, with the above restrictions in place, who engage in disputation over taste, I shall call the "art-interested." And the general thesis of this, and the following two chapters is that the explanation for why people engage in disputes over taste is that they are, for starters, "art-interested," and that they are "art realists" deep down, therefore convinced that they are in possession of art truths; and people who believe they are in possessions of truths *naturally* try to convince others of these truths, no further explanation required.

I will also, into the bargain, be putting up at least a tentative defense of art-realism. But the truth of art-realism, in any or all of its three forms, meaning art realism, aesthetic art-realism, and value art-realism is not essential to my thesis, which merely is that it is the *belief* in art-realism that explains why the art-interested dispute over taste. Whether the belief is true or false is irrelevant to the explanation.

In the present chapter I am concerned with disputes over *interpretational* art-truths: disputes over whether some artwork or other is expressing some proposition or other; disputes, in other words, over meaning. And I will include under the head of "meaning" both propositional meaning and what can be called "representational" meaning. Thus, that it is Icarus represented by that daub of paint is representational meaning, what Breughel the Elder intended to say about the event represented in his *Fall of Icarus* is propositional meaning. (And if you are disturbed about the notion of a picture expressing propositional meaning, choose an example that doesn't disturb you. I will say no more about that.)

So the thesis presently is that the art-interested engage in disputes over taste in the form of disputes over the meaning or meanings of artworks; and the reason they engage in such disputes is, of course, that they are interested in artworks, but, crucially, that they believe the meanings are real properties of the artworks, not "subjective" states of the perceiver, so their reason for entering such disputes is to convince their opponents that the meaning-properties they believe are there are indeed *there*.

Now the reader will recall that I already introduced my take on the meaning of "meaning" in Chapter 7. But the point is important enough to bear repeating as well as amplification.

I adopted, in Chapter 7, Paul Grice's analysis of utterance meaning to serve, as well, for the meanings conveyed by artworks. According to that analysis, as I am employing it, the meaning of an "utterance" whether vocal or textual, or pictorial, is a function *both* of intention and the choice of a viable vehicle for the conveyance of meaning intention. Thus, in Grice's words, "Perhaps we may sum up what is necessary for A to mean something by x as follows: A must intend to induce by x a belief in an audience, and he must also intend his utterance to be recognized as so intended." That is the first condition on meaning. The second is that he must choose a vehicle for conveying his meaning intention that there is "some chance" his audience will recognize as conveying the intended meaning.[1]

But here the following objection might be forthcoming. I have stipulated that those who engage in disputes over taste, the art-interested, range from lay persons with little knowledge of or expertise in the arts, to those learned in such matters. And I have now claimed that the art-interested, so stipulated, dispute over non-aesthetic art relevant properties of artworks, which is to say, *meaning*, because they accept, implicitly or explicitly, a Gricean analysis of meaning. Surely, though, so the objection goes, it is absurd to ascribe to the art-interested at the lower end of the knowledge and expertise scale knowledge of an abstruse analysis of meaning put forward by a philosopher of language, at times, with logical rigor in technical terminology. One may perhaps expect such knowledge of the experts at the high end of the scale; surely not, however, of the man on the street or the woman on the Clapham omnibus.

Well I think the objection is without merit. And here is why.

I suggest that Grice's two-pronged analysis of meaning reflects our pre-systematic intuitions. To begin with, I think it obvious, and uncontentious, that the first Gricean condition on meaning, *intention* to mean, is a pre-systematic intuition; and I think ordinary linguistic usage and ordinary behavior will bear this out. That is why, it appears to me,

---

[1] Paul Grice, *Studies in the Way of Words*, p. 219.

considerable argument is required to convince the laity that authorial intent is irrelevant in determining textual meaning. It is the so-called "intentional fallacy" that is counter-intuitive, not the down-to-earth notion that an utterance can't mean what the utterer could not have intended it to mean.

The second Gricean condition on meaning, though, might plausibly be claimed not to be intuitively grounded, but, rather, a theoretical artifact, and, therefore, not attributable to the lower range of the art-interested. On the contrary, I shall argue, the second Gricean condition on meaning is as intuitive as the first. And I think that is essentially what the conclusion is of that most profound discussion of meaning, in *Through the Looking Glass*, between Alice and Humpty Dumpty. Here, just to remind you, is how the relevant portion of that intriguing colloquy goes.

"I don't know what you mean by 'glory,'" Alice said.

Humpty Dumpty smiled contemptuously. "Of course you don't—till I tell you. I meant 'there's a nice knock-down argument for you'."

"But 'glory' doesn't mean 'a nice knock-down argument'," Alice objected.

"When *I* use a word," Humpty Dumpty said, in a rather scornful tone, "it means just what I choose it to mean—neither more nor less."

"The question is," said Alice, "whether you can make words mean so many different things."

"The question is," said Humpty Dumpty, "which is to be master—that's all."[2]

Now Humpty Dumpty begins, I take it, by appealing to the first Gricean condition: the intuition that intention determines meaning. "When *I* use a word, it means just what I choose it to mean—neither more nor less." Thus, if I say to you, "Meet me at the bank," you may be in doubt whether I meant the riverside or the place where they keep the money. You want to know my intended meaning. And, indeed, Humpty Dumpty would be quite right in averring that in this instance, and in many others like it, words mean what I choose them to mean.

But, of course, the point is that Humpty Dumpty takes this basically sound intuition to an absurd conclusion by ignoring the *limits* on choice of meaning. I can, indeed, *choose* "bank" to mean the riverside *or* the place where they keep the money. I cannot, however, choose it to mean "glory" or "a nice knock-down argument."

[2] Lewis, Carroll, *The Complete Works of Lewis Carroll*, ed. Alexander Woolcott (New York: The Modern Library, n.d.), p. 214.

And that is where Alice's innate common sense kicks in, the common sense, by the way, of a little girl: she has not read Grice! Alice is the voice of common sense in all of her encounters with the mad things that inhabit Wonderland and the world behind the looking glass. Here then Alice brings us back to common sense by perceiving that "The question is whether you can make words mean so many things." The answer, needless to say, is that you cannot. In other words, Alice, the childish voice of pre-systematic intuition and common sense, is enunciating Grice's second condition on meaning. You can't "make words mean so many things" precisely because the second Gricean condition on meaning is that you must choose as a vehicle for conveying your meaning intention something that has "some chance" of conveying that meaning intention to an audience. But "glory" has *no chance* of conveying Humpty Dumpty's intended meaning of "a nice knock-down argument," which is exactly the intuition Alice is evincing in her response to the imperious egg that "The question is whether you can make words mean so many things." She instinctively knows the answer, and it is an emphatic No. You can only "make" words mean what there is "some chance" they can convey.

What I want to suggest, then, with this trip through the looking glass, is that Lewis Carroll was representing as common sense, as intuition, if we will, in the confrontation of Alice with Humpty Dumpty, the second Gricean condition on utterance meaning. And I offer that as evidence that the second Gricean condition on meaning is not a theoretical artifact but, like the first condition, an intuition about utterance meaning shared by the learned and the laity alike; as well, recognized by Lewis Carroll long before it was made philosophy by Paul Grice. Furthermore, I am claiming that the second Gricean condition on utterance meaning, like the first, is (either explicitly or implicitly) assumed by the art-interested, *tout court*, layman to pundit.

Put the two Gricean conditions together, then, for the art-interested, and you get the belief that the non-aesthetic art-relevant properties of artworks, which is to say, their meaning properties, are "objective" properties of artworks and not "subjective" properties "projected" onto them in the way Hume, and later Santayana, thought the property of beauty is projected. It is a matter of fact—and I think Hume and Santayana would agree—that an artist intended an artwork to mean such-and-such and a matter of fact that she fashioned her artwork in such a way that it had, in Grice's words, "some chance" of conveying to her audience her intended meaning.

So the objection that the second Gricean condition on meaning is a theoretical artifact, not a wide-spread intuition, fails. And that being the case, our explanation for why the art-interested dispute over taste regarding non-aesthetic art-relevant properties remains in place. They dispute, of course, because they *are* art-interested, and because they are, deep down, art-realists with regard to non-aesthetic art-relevant properties. And so, like all who believe they are in possession of the truth, they endeavor to convince dissenters, no further motive required.

Perhaps there may be skeptics who doubt whether I really have an accurate picture of "dispute behavior" among the art-interested, with regard to non-aesthetic art-relevant properties. Hume, recall, averred that there were *two* "species" of common sense, *two* opposed intuitions with regard to the beautiful: that there is no disputing about taste, that beauty is in the eye of the beholder, *and* that it really is an objective fact of the matter that one poet is orders of magnitude better than another. And, after all, Kant to the contrary notwithstanding, people do sometimes say, "Beautiful *to you*, maybe, but not *to me*." And are there not, the skeptic may claim, people who demur from a dispute over the meaning of an artwork, shrug their shoulders, and say, "Well, it may mean so-and-so *to you*, but it means such-and-such *to me*."

Of course it is an empirical question as to just what the "disputation behavior" is like among the art-interested with regard to the interpretation of artworks. And I have no rigorous empirical evidence to adduce. All I can offer are the following two personal observations.

First of all, it is my experience that the "*De gustibus...*" shrug is seldom given, among the art-interested, when the *meaning* of artworks is the issue.

But, second, when a dispute over meaning does end in the parties to the dispute throwing up their hands and saying the equivalent of *De gustibus non disputandum est*, you have it your way, I'll have it mine, it means this *to me*, that *to you*, it is my experience, particularly with undergraduates, that the parties can be brought to acknowledge that the dispute has not become irresolvable because it is really a dispute over subjective feelings or attitudes, not "matters of fact." Rather, it is because of an equivocation on the meaning of "meaning," or because, although there *is* a definitive answer to the question, "What does it mean?" the answer happens simply to be inaccessible to us, as frequently *is*, after all, the case in serious, protracted disputes over interpretation.

What I mean by an equivocation over the meaning of "meaning" can best be illustrated with an example. I am going through some old family belongings with a friend of mine looking on, and he asks, picking up a dysfunctional watch, "What are you keeping this piece of junk for?" I reply, somewhat annoyed: "That 'piece of junk,' as you call it, may *mean* nothing *to you*, but it happens to mean a great deal *to me*. It was my father's watch, given him for twenty-five years faithful service at his place of business." In other words, the equivocation is on "meaning," as in "propositional meaning," and "meaning" as in "significance" or "importance." And thus, of course, a work of art may have a different meaning for you from what it has for me, while, nevertheless, meaning what it *means*, and not another thing. (I will be returning to this point later on.)

More frequently, though, I think those skeptical of the notion that what an artwork means is an objective matter of fact are skeptical because they have some real acquaintance with disputes over interpretation of artworks and perceive, quite correctly, that many such disputes are of long standing—think of the Lucy poems!—and seem without prospect of final resolution, as indeed would be the case if the disputes were purely subjective in nature; and thus such skeptics take their seeming intractability to be explained by their subjectivity. Furthermore, in my experience, many of these skeptics take the person defending the objectivity of artistic meaning to be guilty of a kind of *hubris*, being understood to be claiming that he or she *knows* what the meaning of such a disputed artwork is, and being intolerant of divergent interpretations.

But it has been my experience, again, partly with undergraduates, that when the possible equivocation on "meaning" is pointed out it resolves the issue in favor of meaning realism for some skeptics. And, more frequently, when it is pointed out that the intractability of many, or perhaps most disputes over the meanings of artworks does not imply there are not matters of fact at issue, most such skeptics, in my experience, acquiesce in the intuition that artwork meaning *is* a matter of fact. For, after all, there is a perfectly reasonable explanation, if one accepts the Gricean analysis of utterance meaning for works of art, as to why so many disputes over artwork meaning are irresolvable. The intentions of artists, particularly those of the distant past, are notoriously difficult to make out, if not, in the event, totally inaccessible to us now. And so the first Gricean condition on artwork meaning will always be a sticking point, as the history of criticism will surely bear out.

There are of course those whom I have characterized as having a theoretical axe to grind, and whose primary target of opportunity is the first Gricean condition, namely, the artist's intentions. And one's first thought on the matter is that when artists' intentions go, the intuition of the objectivity of meaning goes as well. As E. D. Hirsch put that point, in his vigorous defense of authorial intent as a standard for meaning: "For, once the author had been ruthlessly banished as the determiner of his text's meaning, it very gradually appeared that no adequate principle existed for judging the validity of an interpretation."[3]

Now I have stipulated above that the group of what I have called the art-interested does *not* include those with a theoretical axe to grind, but only those with pre-systematic intuitions in tact about artwork meaning. It might, however, prove enlightening to see whether the intuition, if not the substance of meaning realism survives the rejection of Grice's first condition on utterance meaning. And for starters, it is worth noting that Monroe Beardsley, who, along with William K. Wimsatt, Jr., fired the first shot at the relevance of authorial intent in interpretation, was well known as a staunch defender of the thesis that a literary text has one, and only one correct interpretation. For although he gave up the authority of the author's intention he never gave up the authority of the author's *text*. Meaning realism was alive and well in Beardsley's writings on criticism, the "intentional fallacy" (apparently) to the contrary notwithstanding. Thus with regard to the suggestion that "the literary interpreter . . . has a certain leeway, and does not merely 'report' on 'discovered meaning,' as I said earlier, but puts something of his own into the words; so that different critics may produce different but equally legitimate interpretation, like two sopranos or two ingénues working from the same notations," Beardsley writes: "I find myself rather severe with this line of thought. There is plenty of room for creativity in literary interpretation, if that means thinking of new ways of reading the work, if it means exercising sensitivity and imagination. But the moment the critic begins

---

[3] E. D. Hirsch, *Validity in Interpretation* (New Haven and London: Yale University Press, 1967), p. 3.

to use the work as an occasion for promoting his own ideas, he has abandoned the task of interpretation."[4]

The plot, indeed, thickens with Roland Barthes' celebrated report of the author's demise. At the core of Barthes' argument is the rejection of intention as a criterion of meaning in *literary* texts through, essentially, the rejection of literary artworks as "utterances." Barthes writes, in this regard: "As soon as a fact is narrated no longer with a view to acting directly on reality but intransitively, that is to say, finally outside of any function other than that of the very practice of the symbol itself, this disconnection occurs, *the voice loses its origin*, the author enters into his death, writing begins."[5] I take this rather bombastic statement, shorn of its excess verbiage, to be quite simply telling us that literary texts are not to be taken for or therefore treated as human utterances.

But when a literary text ceases to be an utterance, it, needless to say, ceases to have an utterer, in other words, ceases to have an author. And when it ceases to have an utterer-author, Barthes seems, at least, to be concluding, it ceases to have an interpretation, at least in any recogniz-able form, given what we take the term "interpretation" to mean in the first place. "Once the author is removed," Barthes writes, "the claim to decipher the text becomes quite futile."[6] So, consequently, "every text is eternally written here and now."[7] In other words, I gather, Barthes does indeed take authorial intent as a necessary condition on text interpret-ation, when a text is an utterance. But when it ceases to be an utterance, as literary texts do, then it ceases to have an author, therefore ceases to have an interpretation, or, the way Barthes puts it, deciphering it "becomes quite futile"—"decipher," I take it, being synonymous with "interpret."

Difficult it is to put an intelligible meaning on these gnomic pro-nouncements. But what I make of them leads me to conclude that what we have here comes pretty close to what must constitute some kind of near total subjectivism with regard to textual meaning, where the text in question is a *literary* text. Item: "the claim to decipher the text becomes

[4] Monroe C. Beardsley, *The Possibility of Criticism* (Detroit: Wayne State University Press, 1976), p. 40. And see also p. 44.

[5] Roland Barthes, "The Death of the Author," reprinted in *The Death and Resurrection of the Author*, ed. William Irwin (Westport, CT: Greenwood Press, 2002), p. 3. My italics.

[6] Barthes, "The Death of the Author," p. 6.

[7] Barthes, "The Death of the Author," p. 4.

quite futile." Item: "every text is eternally written here and now." Is there a text at all, one is forced to ponder on, if the text is "written" at every reading? Or is there some way of identifying "the text," in which case "it" has every meaning any reader has ever put on it in the reading? But if so, is that "meaning" at all? I will not go on to multiply the paradoxes any further, although it would be easy enough to do. At the end of the day, however, I think it fair to say that on any reasonable understanding of what artistic realism amounts to, Barthes is not an artistic realist with regard to what I have been calling the non-aesthetic art-relevant properties of artworks, which is to say their meanings.

And it follows directly from Barthes' views on interpretation, I would think, that Barthes, or anyone else who shared his views on this regard would, in ordinary circumstances, have no reason at all to engage in taste-disputation over matters of interpretation: over matters concerning the non-aesthetic art-relevant properties of artworks. For, as I have argued above, the two main explanations for why one disputes are to motivate one's adversary to action, or to convince her of the truth. But by default the former is ruled out as an explanation for all taste-disputes, no matter what the disputants' beliefs. And the latter is ruled out because there seems to be no "truth" of interpretation for the follower of Barthes to believe she is arguing about.

I venture to suggest that the overwhelming majority of the art-interested, as characterized above, would find Barthes' view counter-intuitive in the extreme. Furthermore, there are those who share Barthes' suspicions of authorial intention as a condition on the meaning of artworks, and yet are unwilling to go down the subjectivist road; who, in other words, *do* have a theoretical axe to grind but share the intuition of the art-interested that there are correct and incorrect interpretations: that interpretation isn't just "a matter of taste," but, in fact, "a matter of fact."

One such is, as we have seen, Monroe Beardsley; another Stanley Fish. The latter espouses what appears to be as extreme a subjectivism in matters of interpretation as Barthes': of literary works, he writes, "no reading, however outlandish it might appear, is *inherently* an impossible one."[8]

---

[8] Stanley Fish, *Is There a Text in This Class? The Authority of Interpretive Communities* (Cambridge, MA: Harvard University Press, 1988), p. 347. My italics.

As permissive, however, in the extreme as this avowal appears, Fish is obviously uncomfortable with the prospect of giving up the intuition that some interpretations are right, some wrong, the denial of *inherent impossibility* to the contrary notwithstanding. Thus, he wants to insist that "there are always mechanisms for ruling out readings," but then softens *that* seeming concession to objectivity in interpretation by cautioning that "their source is not the text but the presently recognized interpretive strategies for producing the text"; and those mechanisms, "the canons of acceptability [in interpretation] can change."[9]

This hedging leaves us with the question: On Fish's view is there interpretational "truth" or not? And I think the answer must be that if there is, it is time-relative. Which is to say, it is relative to what mechanisms or canons of correct interpretation happen to be in place *when* the interpretation is given.

For example, assuming Fish's take on interpretation, let us suppose that during the heyday of Romanticism, a poem meant such-and-such, not so-and-so, because the poet intended it to mean such-and-such, not so-and-so, and chose words that had a good chance of conveying his intended meaning; and the interpretational rules in place were, among others, the Gricean conditions on utterance meaning, namely intention and likelihood of the vehicle conveying intended meaning. Suppose though that *now*, in the Beardsley/Fish era, the intention rule and the "likelihood" rule are not in effect, and on the basis of other rules that *now* are in effect, we can, according to these rules, interpret the poem to mean so-and-so, not such-and-such.

In either case, Fish has managed to preserve some sense of correctness in interpretation, which I think was his goal. He wants, in other words, to maintain that in interpretation it will still be something like "business as usual," even under the new dispensation, with no interpretation, no matter how outlandish, *inherently implausible*.[10] But one is forced to wonder (to return to the central question of this book) *what* would motivate someone to dispute over the interpretation of an artwork, if Fish's view of interpretation were correct?

---

[9] Fish, *Is There a Text in This Class?* p. 347.

[10] For more on this, see Peter Kivy, "Fish's Consequences," *British Journal of Aesthetics*, 29 (1989).

There are three possible cases. In the first case, Fish's view of interpretation is correct, but the parties to the dispute are not acquainted
with his view and are arguing in the good old-fashioned way, as art-
interested disputants, with both Gricean intuitions concerning meaning
in place. In this case, of course, it *would* be "business as usual," from the
point of view of the disputants. Both would be art-realists with regard to
art-meaning, and their motivation to dispute would be the usual one: to
convince the other of "the truth"—no further motivation required.
They would both, of course, be mistaken about what they were doing;
but that is irrelevant to the explanation of why they are doing what they
are doing.

In the second possible case, one of the parties to the dispute is a
convert to Fish's view of interpretation while the other is a good old-
fashioned art-realist, with Gricean meaning intuitions. But this case
breaks down into two sub-cases. In the first sub-case, the convert believes
that the Gricean conditions on meaning are, at the present time, in effect
as valid rules of interpretation. In that sub-case, the disputants would be
arguing about the same thing, whether or not the interpretation under
dispute conforms to the artist's intention, although they would, of
course, differ over the status of intention, one thinking it an eternal
verity, the other a changeable rule, here today, gone tomorrow.

In the second sub-case of the second possible case, the convert to Fish
believes that the Gricean conditions on meaning are not in place for
artworks, while his adversary has the good old-fashioned Gricean intuitions. In that sub-case, the dispute would quickly become a dispute not
over the meaning of the artwork but over theories of interpretation. For
the convert to Fish would try, obviously, to convince his adversary that
whether or not the interpretation that began the dispute conforms to the
artist's intentions is completely irrelevant by trying to convert her to
Fish's view of criticism. It is a dispute, now, if it continues, not over the
meaning of an artwork but over critical theory or philosophy of criticism.
In other words, it is not a "dispute over taste," and its *raison d'être* not an
issue in the present study.

Finally, in the third case, *both* parties to the dispute are in Fish's camp.
And the question is do they or do they not agree on which rules for
interpretation are presently in place. Put the case that they agree on the
rules. Then, if they are engaged in a dispute over the meaning of an
artwork, their dispute will be over whether or not, given the rules in

place, those rules do or do not produce the meaning in dispute. And if the rules in place include the Gricean conditions on meaning, then their dispute will be, in part, over whether or not the meaning in dispute was intended by the artist. The dispute would be over the same issue that would be in dispute if the disputants were the art-interested who are in thrall to the Gricean meaning intuitions. But it would, in a sense, be a dispute with weaker motivation, because both parties to it would be operating under the assumption that at any time the "rules" of interpretation could change, and produce an entirely different, even outlandish interpretation.

But now put the case that the disputants share Fish's view of interpretation, but disagree over what rules of interpretation are presently in place, one of the disputants perhaps believing that the "intention rule" is no longer operative, the other believing that it is, the former, therefore, believing that the poem means so-and-so, even though the poet intended such-and-such. In this case, then, it does not seem to be a dispute over interpretation at all, except in an attenuated sense of the word. It is a dispute over *rules*. Furthermore, it is hard to see how such a dispute could be at all protracted, as disputes over interpretation have historically been.

Let me present the thing in a slightly different light. The art-interested, as I have characterized them, share the Gricean intuitions that meaning depends upon intention to mean and the choice of vehicle that has some likelihood of conveying intended meaning to an appropriate audience. Thus when the art-interested engage in a dispute over the meaning of an artwork, it seems as if something deeply important to them is at stake. They are trying to find out what Aeschylus and Dante and Goethe were trying to say to us. Now if, of course, you do not think that is important, then this argument will have no force for you. But if you share with me the feeling of its importance, then I ask you to compare it with the importance, or, as I would put it, the complete lack thereof, if what were at stake were simply whether the temporary rules in place allow us to "make" a text by Aeschylus or Dante or Goethe "mean" such-and-such or so-and-so, or whether one set of rules or another were in fact in place.

I am reminded, here, of the difference between what is at stake in a dispute over the Ptolemaic versus the Copernican world view if you think it is a matter of which account better "saves the appearances," or which account *is true*. Would Galileo have been shown the instruments of "persuasion" if he had not made it a matter of *the truth*? (And, some have asked, would there have been a "scientific revolution" if it were merely saving the appearances, not truth at stake?)

Thus, I guess what I am saying is that Fish may save the appearance of disputes over interpretation but not the reality. Yes, if you share Fish's view there is, for you, "truth" in interpretation, as there would not be if you were in Barthes' camp. It does not, however, save the intuition that Aeschylus and Dante and Goethe and all the others were telling us things, and what they were telling us is deeply important for us to know.

Yet, in the event, whether or not Fish saved the appearance of truth in interpretation is beside the point. For I am concerned with the art-interested, not Fish and his followers, who have an axe to grind. And the art-interested, when one makes crystal clear to them what the implications really are of Fish's view will, I suggest, reject it as counter-intuitive in the extreme, as they would the views of Barthes.

One further point, perhaps, can be advanced in Fish's favor. As we saw, it follows that on his view an artwork either has as many meanings as the rules of engagement will permit at any given time, even if they are incompatible with one another, or one meaning at one time, another meaning at another time, as the rules of engagement change over time. And at first glance, at least, these implications may seem innocuous enough to the art-interested. For in the marketplace, it seems, "common sense" has it that, of course, an artwork of the past "means" something to us, perhaps, that it couldn't have "meant" to the artist's contemporaries, so, of course, its meaning changes over time. As well, it is a truism in the marketplace that one of the things that makes works of art so special is that each has a myriad, almost inexhaustible, variety of different meanings, unlike, say, a passage of expository prose. In this respect, artworks are "rich in meaning."

However, both of these marketplace clichés, in my experience, are quickly made to be seen as simply misleading ways of stating truths about artworks that imply neither their having multiple, perhaps incompatible meanings, nor their meaning *changing* over time. And when this is made clear, what emerges is that the art-interested, who do not have an axe to grind, generally share the intuitions that intention to mean is a necessary condition on meaning, and that, therefore, when the artist succeeds in meaning what she intends to mean, that is what the artwork means, then, now, and forever: one objective truth.

What, then, do these clichés signify? Clearly, the truism to the effect that an artwork's meaning changes over time is a misleading way of saying, what is undoubtedly true, that its significance or relevance changes over time. Thus an artwork may *gain* significance for us that perhaps it did not have for its contemporaries because events have transpired in *our* lifetimes on which it may shed light. Contrariwise, it may lose relevance for us because the world view it projects is no longer a real option for us, or because the moral issue it addresses has for us been resolved. Its significance for us has changed. But its meaning has not. And the two are easily conflated, as we have already seen.

As for the truism that works of art, particularly complex, important ones, are characterized by being rich, indeed inexhaustible in multiple meanings, it should not be confused, as I think it frequently is, with the valid assertion that such works are susceptible of numerous contestable interpretations, frequent new and novel interpretations, with little prospect for consensus. But the latter truism neither implies nor is equivalent to the former one. Which is to say, that there are numerous conflicting interpretations of complex artworks, and that we may never know which is the correct one, if any, seems an intuitively correct claim, and is not to be confused with the highly unintuitive, and, on the face of it, false claim that there are numerous conflicting interpretations of complex artworks, all of which are correct.

My conclusion then is that the art-interested generally share the intuition that many—not necessarily all—artworks have propositional or representational meaning, fulfilling the two Gricean conditions on meaning: that the meaning be intended by the artist, and that the artist has chosen a means of conveying his or her meaning intention that has some palpable likelihood of conveying that meaning intention to a competent audience. The intuition is that the non-aesthetic art-relevant "property" of meaning is a real, robust property of those artworks that possess it. The art-interested, then, are generally "art-realists" when it comes to the non-aesthetic art-relevant property of artistic meaning.

One further point, and an important point, before we get on.

The object of the exercise is to explain why we dispute over taste, which is to say, why we dispute over interpretation of artworks. My explanation is that the art-interested dispute over interpretation simply because they are art-realists with regard to artistic meaning and, therefore, believe they are in possession of the truth about artistic meaning, motive enough, no further motive required.

Note once again that it is only necessary for my argument that the art-interested *believe* art realism to be true as regards art-meaning. There is no requirement that the belief be true. But, as a matter of fact, I have been arguing that it *is* true. And it might be well to nail this point down by observing that the major problem usually associated with moral realism, and its poor relation, what might be called "aesthetic realism," is absent from what I have been calling artistic realism with regard to the non-aesthetic art-relevant property of art-meaning.

The prima facie problem for the moral realist, ostensibly an ontological problem, is how to find moral properties, which is to say, value properties, in a universe of "atoms in the void." This problem of "moral metaphysics," as Shafer-Landau describes it, is well-put by Shafer-Landau in the following way:

What kind of a thing could a value be? This is an especially difficult question for moral realists, given a currently popular view about the kinds of things that can plausibly count as occupants of our world. This view claims that things exist independently of our say so only if such things figure in the best (extant or possible) scientific theories. But moral truths cannot be confirmed scientifically. We don't bump into them, we can't taste or touch them.[11]

Now I am not suggesting that there is no problem about the metaphysical status of "meaning" in a universe of atoms in the void. There is, of course, and it is for metaphysics and philosophy of language to work out. But what I am suggesting is that there is no *special* problem about artistic realism with regard to artistic meaning, as there is about moral realism. Artistic meaning is just a species of meaning *uberhaupt*. It presents no further metaphysical problem, just because it is *artistic* meaning, than meaning itself may present. And no one, I do not think, thinks that "meaning realism" is somehow inconsistent with the scientific world view.

Of course when we come to aesthetic realism, and art-value realism, we will, indeed, find, rearing its ugly head, a near relation of the problem of moral metaphysics. But that is a subject for the succeeding chapters. So it is time now to close the present one by stating yet again its final conclusions.

---

[11] Shafer-Landau, *Moral Realism*, p. 3.

It is my contention that those I have characterized as the art-interested actively and vigorously engage in disputation over the interpretation of works of art, which is to say, their non-aesthetic art-relevant properties—their meaning properties. What motivates these disputes is not, as in many moral disputes, the desire to initiate appropriate actions, but, rather, the conviction on the part of the parties to such disputes that they are in possession of the truth and the desire to bring others to possess the truth as well. They are, in other words, art-realists with regard to non-aesthetic art-relevant, meaning properties of artworks, and being realists in this regard are motivated to get others to acknowledge the existence of the properties of artworks which they firmly believe they have. And whether or not their belief in this form of art-realism is true, it is enough that they *have* the belief to explain why, in this case, we dispute over taste.

It remains, then, for us to now go on to an examination of disputes over the aesthetic qualities of artworks, and disputes over their value. And with regard to them, the issue of realism becomes thornier, as we shall see.

13

The Truth of Analysis

It is common parlance in the literary and representational arts, I think, to use the word "interpretation" to denote the spelling out of meaning. And I have so used it in the previous chapter.

The word "analysis," on the other hand, when used in an artistic context, most commonly, I think, occurs as a description of an activity in professional musical circles that consists in elucidating the harmonic, contrapuntal, and formal structure of musical works without text, which is to say, absolute music, or, if the subject is music with a text, the elucidation, as above, of the *musical* part of the work.

This is not to say that the term "interpretation" does not occur in musical discourse. Most frequently it is used in musical discourse to refer to a *performance*, as when a critic describes a particular pianist's performance of Beethoven's *Hammerklavier* Sonata as her "interpretation" of the work. And there *are* those—I not among them—who put literary or representational interpretations on works of the absolute music repertory. However, because "analysis" is a term so closely associated with elucidation of the pure musical parameters, and not with elucidation of propositional or representational meaning in the arts, I have decided, for the purposes of the present study, to reserve the term "interpretation" *exclusively* for the elucidation of propositional and representational meaning, as I have done in the previous chapter, and "analysis" *exclusively* for the elucidation of the non-meaning, aesthetic, art-relevant properties of artworks, as I will in the present one. Furthermore, I will be using the term "analysis" not merely to refer to the elucidation of the aesthetic properties of musical works, from which I have kidnapped the term, but to refer to the elucidation of the aesthetic properties of any artwork that may have them. This now leaves me, of course, with the task of explaining just *what* exactly I mean by the "aesthetic" properties or features of artworks. And I undertake that task now.

The notion of artworks, and other "objects" possessing "aesthetic" properties or features is of course not new. The term "aesthetic" was coined by Alexander Baumgarten in the early eighteenth century; and by the close of that century such features of artworks, such as the beautiful, the sublime, and the picturesque would have been called, at least by some, "aesthetic" features. Furthermore, I dare say that even in classical antiquity, although lacking the term, Plato, Aristotle, and the Roman writers on art, particularly poetry, had the concept, or something like it, and described works of art in what *we* would call "aesthetic" terms.

However that may be, the issue of "aesthetic" properties, in their myriad varieties, their "ontology" and "epistemology," entered contemporary philosophical thought, in 1959, through Frank Sibley's ground-breaking article, "Aesthetic Concepts," which, it is fair to say, defined my own early career in aesthetics, and the careers of many other young philosophers of art as well.[1]

My own work on Sibley's account of what he called "aesthetic concepts" culminated in my first book, *Speaking of Art*, in which I launched an extended argument against Sibley's controversial and much discussed claim that aesthetic concepts were, as he put it, non-condition-governed.[2] I shall have more to say a bit later on concerning Sibley's claim that aesthetic concepts are not condition-governed. My point here however is merely to get clear about what I shall call, not aesthetic concepts but, rather, aesthetic properties or features, although I rather think this is merely a matter of notation, not of substance.

A good beginning, I think, would be to quote part of the passage in which Sibley introduces aesthetic concepts to us. He writes:

We say that a novel has a great number of characters and deals with life in a manufacturing town; that a painting uses pale colors, and has kneeling figures in the foreground; that the theme in a fugue is inverted at such a point and that there is a stretto at the close; that the action of a play takes place in the span of one day and that there is a reconciliation scene in the fifth act.... On the other hand, we also say that a poem is tightly knit or deeply moving; that a picture lacks balance or has a certain serenity and repose, or that the grouping of the figures sets up an exciting tension; that the characters in a novel never really come to life, or that a certain episode strikes a false note.[3]

---

[1] Sibley, "Aesthetic Concepts."
[2] See Peter Kivy, *Speaking of Art* (The Hague: Martinus Nijhoff, 1973).
[3] Sibley, "Aesthetic Concepts," p. 63.

THE TRUTH OF ANALYSIS 121

The former features of artworks are "non-aesthetic" features, the latter "aesthetic" ones. What differentiates them? Two things, on Sibley's view.

First, as Sibley puts it, with regard to the latter, aesthetic features, "It would be natural enough to say that the making of such judgments as these requires the exercise of taste, perceptiveness, or sensitivity, of aesthetic discrimination or appreciation; one would not say that of my first group."[4] But second, and what became the point of extended controversy in the wake of Sibley's article, application of aesthetic terms, as opposed to non-aesthetic ones, as Sibley described it, was "non-condition-governed." Which is to say, "There are no sufficient conditions, no non-aesthetic features such that the presence of some set or numbers of them will beyond question logically justify or warrant the application of an aesthetic term."[5]

Now I have no intention of reviving, here, the various issues surrounding this highly controversial, and much discussed claim of Sibley's. I had my innings in 1973 and have nothing more to say about the matter at this late date. My aim, rather, is to use Sibley's examples of aesthetic and non-aesthetic features as a jumping off place for my characterization of what I take to be aesthetic features of artworks and the nature of "aesthetic realism."

Let me point out, for starters, how odd it would seem to someone even casually conversant with art-talk to be told that theme-inversion and stretto in a fugue, or a reconciliation scene in a play are not "aesthetic" features of the works. I side with the "casually conversant" on this point and will, therefore, be construing the class of "aesthetic" features of artworks far more broadly than Sibley, to include features such as stretto or inversion in a fugue, and a reconciliation scene in a plot, as well as those that Sibley characterizes as "aesthetic" features, such as balance, serenity, being tightly knit, and so on.

Furthermore, I shall distinguish between Sibley's first set of artistic features, and his second set, not by claiming the second set requires "taste' or some special faculty for perception, nor by claiming that the first set are condition-governed, the second set non-condition-governed, as Sibley does. For both of these claims are highly controversial; and, indeed, as I have argued elsewhere at length, I take them to be false.[6]

---

[4] Sibley, "Aesthetic Concepts," p. 57.   [5] Sibley, "Aesthetic Concepts," pp. 67–8.
[6] On this, see Kivy, *Speaking of Art, passim.*

The distinction I *do* wish tentatively to make between them is relatively uncontroversial: namely, that between non-evaluative and evaluative descriptions. Clearly, saying that a fugue has a stretto at its close, or that there is a reconciliation scene in the fifth act of a play is to offer a description that conveys no value judgment. There are strettos in poor fugues as well as great ones, and reconciliation scenes in poor plays as well as great ones. Furthermore, there are well-brought-off strettos and reconciliation scenes and there are clumsy inept ones. In other words, one does not necessarily praise a fugue by pointing out that it has a stretto at its close or necessarily praise a play for having a reconciliation scene in the fifth act.

I said that I am making this distinction tentatively. For in the end I am going to qualify it somewhat and, as well, offer what I take to be a more logically rigorous distinction between the first and second set of what I am calling "aesthetic features" of artworks. But more of that anon.

In any case, in contrast, the aesthetic features in Sibley's second set are *clearly* aesthetic value-features; so to ascribe any one of them to an artwork is, *ipso facto*, to pass a negative or positive judgment, not necessarily a blanket one. For, obviously, an artwork can be a bad one even though it might possess the positive quality of being tightly knit, or a good one even though it might possess the negative quality of lacking balance.

Sibley's second set of aesthetic concepts, then, might be called "thick" aesthetic value concepts, as opposed to "thin" ones. That is, they are both evaluative and descriptive. Thus if I say that a dance was "graceful" I not only pass a positive evaluation on it but convey information about what it was like. Whereas if I say that it was "good" I pass a positive value judgment on it but no further information.

But here a caveat, in the form of a qualification, must be entered. What I am claiming about evaluative aesthetic features is, more accurately, to appropriate a phrase from moral theory, that they are *prima facie* either positive or negative in valence. Thus, keeping promises, telling the truth (i.e. not lying), and returning what you borrowed all have, *in general,* positive moral valence, which it is to say, it is, *in general,* the right thing to do to keep promises, tell the truth, and return what you have borrowed.

But, clearly, there are circumstances in which it would be wrong to keep a promise, wrong to tell the truth, wrong to return what you borrowed. If you promise to meet me for lunch and keep your promise, instead of saving a child from drowning, if you tell a Gestapo officer that you are hiding a Jew in your attic, when he asks, to avoid lying, and, to use Plato's age-old example, if you return a sword to a man from whom you have borrowed it, who has subsequently gone mad, you are doing the wrong thing if you keep your promise, the wrong thing if you tell the truth, the wrong thing if you return what you borrowed.

In a like manner, what I am calling aesthetic value features are prima facie positive or negative in artistic valence. Thus, *in general*, being balanced, tightly knit, and so forth, are good-making features of artworks. But there can be instances in which such would turn out to have a negative artistic valence. So in what follows, when I refer to aesthetic value terms and features, they must be understood as prime facie aesthetic value terms, in the sense of prima facie just explained.

But the question might well arise with regard to a very populous class of aesthetic properties I have not yet mentioned, namely *expressive* properties of artwork, as to whether *they* are evaluative or non-evaluative. And let me emphasize here, that by expressive properties I mean those "in" the artwork, not the dispositional properties for making us (say) sad, or happy, and so on, which I consider artistic properties, though not aesthetic ones.[7] One's first, non-reflective response would likely be that they are purely descriptive, non-evaluative aesthetic properties. After all, a work can be sad and bad.

I think, however, that this initial response is off the mark. For my experience with the critical literature in the arts strongly suggests that, generally speaking, when an expressive property is ascribed to an art work, the ascription amounts to a positive evaluation: to praise. When the critic remarks, "How profoundly melancholy!" and the like, such remarks carry a distinctly positive connotation, to my mind, under usual circumstances.

---

[7] On this, see Peter Kivy, *Once-Told Tales: An Essay in Literary Aesthetics* (Chichester: Wiley Blackwell, 2011), Chapters 3 and 4. It is thus highly misleading to claim, as Alan Goldman seems to be doing, that I think "expressive properties are not aesthetically relevant." Alan H. Goldman, *Philosophy and the Novel* (Oxford: Oxford University Press, 2013), p. 4, and p. 4, n. 2. Dispositional expressive properties I claim are artistically relevant but not aesthetic properties, non-dispositional properties I claim to be both aesthetic and artistically relevant.

However, like other evaluative aesthetic properties I have mentioned, their value is defeasible, which is to say, can be defeated by context. Thus, to adduce some examples, the serenely joyous quality of Gluck's aria for Orfeo, *Che faro Euridice*, mourning the death of Euridice, a notorious case, has been frequently put down as an aesthetic defect, because of its incongruity with the sentiment expressed in the text. As Alfred Einstein has remarked, "Critics have thought it strange . . . that *this* aria should be in C major and might as well express the opposite meaning."[8] Or consider this couplet of Shelley's:

> Death is here, death is there,
> Death is busy everywhere.

How spritely and gay it is, rhythmically. Yet, of course, this spritely and gay rhythm is a defect because inconstant with the subject matter.

Thus I put expressive properties of artworks squarely in the class of evaluative aesthetic properties, although that position, I grant, is arguable. And I see no reason to think they constitute a problem for me.

There are, then, "aesthetic features," as I am using that phrase, which are, so to speak, evaluatively neutral aesthetic features of artworks, and aesthetic features of artworks that have either positive or negative evaluative valence. And one might, of course, be an aesthetic realist with regard to one kind but not the other. However, before we get to that issue, I must further clarify what I take the *aesthetic* features of artworks specifically to be.

I take it that all aesthetic features of artworks, both the non-value and the value features, are, to put it one way, art-relevant structural and phenomenological features of them. And these features are, of course, the subject of "analysis," as I am using that term. Thus "interpretation" is the explication of what an artwork means, if it means anything, "analysis" an explication of how the artwork "works," what makes it tick. That what an artwork means, and how it works, what makes it tick, are intimately related one with the other hardly requires argument.

We are now ready to return to the subject of this monograph: Why is there disputing over taste? And in the present chapter the special case of that question is, of course: Why do we dispute over matters of aesthetics,

---

[8]   Alfred Einstein, *Gluck*, trans. Eric Blom (London: J. M. Dent; New York: E. P. Dutton, 1954), p. 82.

in the meaning of "aesthetic" I have specified here? Why do we dispute over the analysis of artworks? Which is to say: Why do we argue over whether a given artwork does or does not possess such-and-such an aesthetic property?

Perhaps, though, we have moved too quickly. I have assumed, obviously, in asking the question: Why do we argue over whether artworks possess this or that aesthetic feature? That we *do* so argue. But *do* we? And the answer, I suspect, is "Yes and No."

The answer is No, I think, for what I have been calling "non-evaluative" aesthetic features, a great deal of the time. That is simply because whether or not an artwork possesses one of them is clear-cut. There is nothing to dispute or disagree *about*. If there is a stretto at the close of a fugue, it is there for all to hear. If there is a reconciliation scene in the fifth act, it is there for all to see. And in such cases it is the critic's role not to argue with someone that they are there but merely to point out to the non-perceiver *that* they are there and, if necessary, explain to the non-perceiver what a stretto or reconciliation scene *is*.

But I did say that this is so "a great deal of the time"; and that way of putting it was no accident. For sometimes, whether or not an artwork possesses a non-evaluative aesthetic feature *can* be a matter of dispute. Let me adduce an example.

As my musical readers will know, one of the tricks of the classical composer's trade is known as melodic inversion, described by the *Harvard Dictionary of Music* in this wise: "A melody (subject) is inverted when each ascending interval is changed into the corresponding descending interval and vice versa."[9] The device occurs, of course, frequently in fugue, but elsewhere as well. And usually it is obvious to the experienced ear because the inverted theme occurs hard by the original theme so that the relationship between the two is immediately perceived.

However, an interesting case occurs in Beethoven's great C-sharp minor Quartet where it is debatable whether or not it is a case of inversion. The first movement of the quartet begins fugally. And the main theme of the finale, which enters in the second measure, appears to be an inversion, although not literal, of the fugue subject that begins the quartet. As Joseph Kerman puts it, in his universally admired study of

---

[9] Don Michael Randel (ed.), *The Harvard Dictionary of Music* (Cambridge, MA, and London: Belknap Press of Harvard University Press, 1978), p. 239.

the Beethoven quartets: "without duplicating the original fugue subject, the [finale] theme retraces its line, performs a sort of inversion or transformation upon it."[10]

Notice Kerman's apparent diffidence in the matter. The finale theme is "a sort of inversion." Is it an inversion of the fugue theme of the first movement or not? Obviously Kerman does not think it is a certainty. And that leaves it open to dispute. After all, the middle movements of the work stand between the opening fugue and the finale. Are we really meant to hear the thematic relationship of inversion between them as we would if they occurred cheek by jowl in a fugue where inversion of the fugue subject is a standard compositional procedure?

Here then is a case where it is *disputable* whether or not a non-evaluative aesthetic feature is or is not possessed by the artwork. But what exactly would the disputants in such an argument be disputing *about*?

One obvious answer would be that they are arguing over the simple matter of fact as to whether the notes in the finale theme do or do not satisfy the conditions for inversion, as stipulated, for example, by the *Harvard Dictionary* definition: "each ascending interval is changed into the corresponding descending interval and vice versa." But matters are not that simple.

Given that the finale theme comes close enough to the *Harvard Dictionary* definition of an inversion of the fugue subject, one can *hear it as* the fugue subject inverted. The question, though, is *should* we so hear it? And I take it that the answer to that question devolves on Beethoven's *intention*. In other words, I do not believe there can be *accidental* inversion.

The reason for this claim, as I have argued elsewhere, is that theme inversion, and various other compositional techniques like it, that constitute many of the non-evaluative aesthetic features of musical works in the classical music repertory, are products of musical craft, or skill, if you like.[11] And part of our appreciation of them, and other such features in the various arts, is appreciation of the skill or craft that they require.

---

[10] Joseph Kerman, *The Beethoven Quartets* (New York: Alfred A. Knopf, 1967), p. 343.

[11] On this, see Peter Kivy, "Authorial Intention and the Pure Musical Parameters," in Kivy, *Sounding Off: Eleven Essays in the Philosophy of Music* (Oxford: Oxford University Press, 2012).

Hence, if there is such a feature whose presence in an artwork is in dispute, the dispute is ultimately over whether the feature is "accidental" or intended. And that clearly is a matter of fact, one way or the other. Thus on the infrequent occasion when there is dispute over whether a work of art possesses some non-evaluative feature or other, we have a pretty clear explanation for why it is engaged in. There seems good reason for believing that those engaged in the dispute either explicitly or implicitly are aware that they are disputing over a matter of fact: whether or not the work of art possesses the non-evaluative feature in dispute, which devolves on two further matters of fact: whether the feature in dispute has enough of the properties such a feature must have to qualify as the feature, and whether the feature was intended by the artist to be there—was a product of the artist's craft or skill, not merely unintended. No problem here.

However, it is here that I want to enter the disclaimer I mentioned I would at the outset of my attempt to distinguish between the first and second set of aesthetic features. And the disclaimer is this. Many of the features in the first set which Sibley denominates non-aesthetic and I aesthetic features of artworks do not seem to require skill or craft for their presence. But some do, inversion or stretto or reconciliation scenes. And the skill or craft that we admire when we detect their presence is clearly a *value*. So no matter how ill brought off they may be they *do* constitute at least some modicum of aesthetic value to the works in which they appear. So it seems to follow that describing artworks in terms of them *is* ipso facto positively evaluating them. Nevertheless, it would seem that their presence does not pose any peculiar, ontological problem. It is a *fact* that they are there, and there's an end on it.

But when we get to the thick evaluative aesthetic descriptions, such as "balanced," "graceful," and "beautiful" and "sublime" (in their thick evaluative sense) matters are not so straightforward. For *value* has raised its ugly head.

Let me begin with a matter of terminology which is at the same time a matter of some substance. The philosophical issue of "moral realism," as it is presently described, is, of course, in its most general sense, as old as philosophy itself. But in its contemporary incarnation, which is the only form of it I will take to be relevant to my discussion here, it is briefly described by Shafer-Landau this way: "At the simplest level, all [moral] realists embrace the idea that there is a moral reality that people are trying to represent when they make judgements about what is right and wrong. The disagreements that arise among realists primarily have to do with the nature of this reality."[12]

To be noted straightaway is that moral realism, as Shafer-Landau characterizes it, is concerned with the "moral reality" of "right and wrong," the two operative predicates in moral judgments. And they are both, one assumes, "thin" value judgments that convey no descriptive information, as, for example, the moral predicates "courageous" and "cowardly" would do.

And it is my experience that in the rare instances in which an ethicist refers to "aesthetic realism"—and they *are* rare—they have the same thin sense in mind of what is being referred to in aesthetic judgments. "Beautiful," clearly used in its thin sense, as a general term of "aesthetic" evaluation, is the term almost invariably adduced.

I think it is seldom that an ethicist has any real knowledge of or interest in matters of philosophical aesthetics. Whereas it is far more common for an aesthetician to have knowledge of and interest in moral philosophy. I am not passing some sort of invidious judgment on ethicists. I am simply stating a matter of fact the reasons for which I have no interest in exploring or conjecturing about here. My only point is that because of this lack of interest in aesthetics on the part of moral philosophers they tend not to realize the complexity of what aesthetic realism as a philosophical position would be. It is not simply a matter of "aesthetic," for which most of the time read "artistic," value realism, but aesthetic realism across the board: value realism as it might apply to the whole range of thick aesthetic value terms. Thus it might be that whereas aesthetic value realism *simpliciter*, that is, realism vis-à-vis the goodness or badness of artworks, is implausible, aesthetic realism with regard to thick aesthetic value terms such as "unified," "balanced," "graceful," and so forth, is not. In other words, it behooves us to give the two forms of aesthetic reality separate hearings. And that is what I intend to do in this chapter and the next.

But first of all, we return to our central question, *Cur de gustibus disputandum est?* now having in mind disputes over evaluative aesthetic features. That the art-interested *do* dispute over the presence or absence

---

[12] Shafer-Landau, *Moral Realism*, p. 18.

of such features seems itself indisputable. When the art-interested, either at the low end of the expertise scale, or the high end, or in between, congregate after seeing a movie or play, or after reading a novel in a book club, or standing before a painting in a museum, they surely do converse about what they have experienced. And they surely do not simply say "I liked it" or "I didn't," "It's good," or "It isn't." They may indeed say all of these things. They will not, however, leave it at that, usually, if they *are* the art-interested, and if they do disagree. They will try to convince others of their judgments. And to do that they will inevitably affirm or deny the presence or absence of aesthetic value features in the artworks in dispute.

Thus, two members of a book club disagree about the merits of a novel they have just read. The party of the first part passes a negative judgment on it because he found the plot "confused" and "chaotic." But the party of the second part, *au contraire*, passes a positive judgment because she experienced the plot as possessing "organic unity" in something like the Aristotelian sense. They are arguing over whether the plot does or does not possess the aesthetic value feature, the aesthetic good-making property of organic unity. And they each cite other features of the plot that either detract from, or contribute to the plot's organic unity.

Why dispute the point rather than just give the "aesthetic shrug"? As I have repeatedly argued, it cannot be for the purpose of motivating one's opponent to action. The conclusion of a moral argument may be a moral imperative. But there seem to be no analogous aesthetic imperatives at the conclusions of aesthetic arguments. And that leaves us, yet again, with the conclusion that the parties to the kind of dispute over taste now on the table are arguing about what they take to be a matter of fact. They are *realists* with regard to evaluative aesthetic properties. In the present case, they are realists with regard to the feature of organic unity, which the party of the first part thinks the plot of the novel does not possess, and the party of the second part insists that it does. They are not in the mode of "It's organically unified *to you*, perhaps, but not *to me*," which, after all, sounds odd, at least as odd as "It's blue *to you*, not *to me*," if not "It's X *to you*, not *to me*," where X is an ordinary matter of fact.

Now I am in no way launching some kind of "ordinary language" argument to the effect that realism with regard to evaluative aesthetic properties must be true, although it *is*, after all, the kind of argument which moral realists sometimes use as step one in their arguments to moral realism. For all that is necessary for explaining why the art-interested engage in disputes over evaluative aesthetic properties of artworks is that they *believe* they are arguing about the real properties of artworks. Their belief may be false, as the aesthetic "error theorist" will insist. But as long as they hold the belief it explains why they do dispute rather than give the aesthetic shrug. "The truth" is motive enough.

Nevertheless, the ardent philosophical inquirer will not be satisfied with such a weak conclusion, but will want to push inquiry to the bitter end and determine not only that the belief of the art-interested in the reality of evaluative aesthetic features is in place but whether it is a *true* belief. Is aesthetic realism with regard to evaluative aesthetic features a plausible position?

It is agreed on all hands that moral realism presents serious problems. And I have already alluded to perhaps the most pressing one, the metaphysical problem, in the previous chapter, of meaning in the arts. I suggested there that realism with regard to *meaning* in the arts, presented no special metaphysical problem beyond whatever metaphysical problems meaning in general might present. But what about realism with regard to evaluative aesthetic features? Do *they* raise a metaphysical problem?

First let me address the following metaphysical problem that Shafer-Landau claims must be met by the moral realist. "We believe in the existence of the entities we do because they play a role in causing observable phenomena."[13] But moral "facts" do not seem to satisfy this condition.

To be noticed straightaway about evaluative aesthetic features is that they seem, unlike moral facts, to be perfectly straightforward perceptual or "experiential" properties. Their "phenomenology" seems right, unproblematic, in this respect, for real properties in the external world.

I distinguished above between perceptual and experiential evaluative aesthetic properties. So let me make that distinction clear before I continue.

In both the visual and the aural arts it appears uncontroversial that, whatever their ontological status, evaluative aesthetic features are *perceived* in the quite literal sense of the word, as in external perception. We

---

[13] Shafer-Landau, *Moral Realism*, p. 83.

see them or we *hear* them. We see the balance or tension in a painting and we see the graceful movements of the ballerina on point. We hear the organic unity of the symphony's first movement and we hear the eloquence of the actor's soliloquy. We see and hear these features as features of the works or performances: as inhering "in" them like the color of an orange or the timbre of the oboe's sound.

But of course there are artworks which we do not literally perceive in the literal sense of see or hear: novels, of course, and poetry, when it is not recited but silently read. In such cases, perhaps, the appropriate word for our awareness of their evaluative aesthetic features is "experience," although "perceive," in its more general sense, is not, I suppose, totally inappropriate. So let us say, then, that I "experience" the organic unity of a novel's plot, or the lyric quality of a poem, and so forth. In some reasonable sense or other of "perceive," we can be said to perceive such evaluative aesthetic features of these neither seen nor heard artworks as, as well, the mathematician is said to "perceive" the elegance, an evaluative aesthetic feature, in some mathematical proof. And it surely does seem as if, in these cases, we are experiencing the aesthetic properties as "in" the artworks in as robust a sense as the sense in which we experience such properties "in" artworks we see and hear.

So it appears to me that with regard to Shafer-Landau's contention that "We believe in the existence of the entities we do because they play a role in causing observable phenomena," evaluative aesthetic properties seem to come off pretty well. They do, indeed, "play a role in causing observable phenomena," and in a far more obvious way than do "moral facts." In this regard they seem altogether viable candidates for a realistic interpretation. They are "entities" we believe in the real existence of "because they play a role in causing observable phenomena."

But now the question naturally arises as to what *kinds* of "entities" evaluative aesthetic properties *are*. And a tempting though controversial answer, which I want briefly to consider here, is that they are "emergent entities." In making this suggestion I will be relying on, as far as I know, the most recent attempt in the literature to clarify and defend this troublesome concept of emergent qualities, namely, the article, "Emergence and Fundamentality," by Elizabeth Barnes.[14]

---

[14] Elizabeth Barnes, "Emergence and Fundamentality," *Mind*, 121 (2012).

Barnes's concise characterization of "emergentism" is as follows: "Emergentists maintain that the parts of a system, through their collective activity, can sometimes give rise to an entity which is quite distinct—in terms of its structure, its causal powers, its ontological makeup, etc.—from the parts of the system, or from anything these parts compose."[15]

Needless to say, the concept of emergent properties has a long and troubled history, and the nature of these properties, as well as their very existence, has been, and remains highly debatable. As Barnes observes: "Things get tricky, though, when we try to understand exactly what is meant by the notion of emergence. It is often couched in metaphors . . . and it is not clear how to cash those metaphors out."[16]

Nevertheless, in spite of its difficulties, emergence seems a likely prospect, even intuitive, for the ontology of evaluative aesthetic properties. For one thing, it is clear that the evaluative aesthetic properties of artworks exist in virtue of *other* features, on which they supervene and to which we point or allude to in defending our ascriptions of evaluative aesthetic features to artworks. We say that an artwork is graceful or balanced or possesses organic unity *because* it has this set of features or that, which *makes* it graceful or balanced or unified.

But, furthermore, I do not think that we take evaluative aesthetic features to merely "reduce to" the features by virtue of which we say they obtain. They are something over and beyond the features on which they may supervene. At least that is how I experience them, and I think others I have talked with do. Indeed, if one were in the process of explaining emergence to the uninitiated, I imagine that evaluative aesthetic features would likely be some that would immediately come to mind as illustrative examples, since aesthetic experience is so widespread and familiar. They would appear to be paradigm cases of emergent entities, if such entities do in fact exist, not problematic or peripheral ones.

Now, though, we have to consider the more logically rigorous distinction I promised earlier between the first and second set of aesthetic qualities. It is simply that the former are assuredly *not* emergent entities, whereas the latter arguably *are*. To be a "stretto" or an "inversion" or reconciliation scene is not to be something new, over and above the features that it describes. Whereas to be "balanced" or "graceful" or

---

[15] Barnes, "Emergence and Fundamentality," p. 873.
[16] Barnes, "Emergence and Fundamentality," p. 874.

"organically unified" is, I am claiming, to be a "new" entity, supervening on the entities on which it depends and from which it "emerges."

The metaphysics of emergent entities is a long and nasty business. And I am not qualified, nor would it be either useful or necessary, if I were, to go into the matter in excruciating detail. But in her extremely exacting article, Professor Barnes makes two important claims about the ontological status of emergent entities that can be stated briefly and that *are* relevant to present concerns.

Barnes's "central thesis is this," as she puts it:"that there is ontological emergence is the claim that some things which are fundamental are not ontologically independent."[17] Obviously the two operative concepts here are *fundamentality* and *ontological dependence*. And the two important claims I referred to just now that Barnes is making about the ontological status of emergent entities devolve on these two concepts.

Ontological dependence is understood by Barnes in this wise: x is ontologically dependent if and only if "in any situation in which there is something exactly like x, you've got to have other things existing alongside it. You cannot have x by itself. And in that sense, x depends (at every moment of its existence) on other things."[18]

The first claim, then, is that emergent entities, as has already become obvious from my remarks about evaluative aesthetic properties, are dependent entities. They depend for their existence upon the existence of other things from which they "emerge," on which they supervene. And this of course is true of evaluative aesthetic properties as well, if indeed they are, as I am suggesting, emergent entities.

The concept of *fundamentality* Barnes explicates in the following theological metaphor: "the fundamental entities are all and only those entities which God needs to create in order to make the world how it is. So if God wants to create a world w, the fundamental entities will be the entities necessary and sufficient for God to create in order for her creation to count as a creation of w."[19]

Now given this characterization of the fundamental entities, the surprising conclusion seems to follow that some *dependent* entities are *fundamental* entities, namely, *emergent* entities. As Barnes explains:

[17] Barnes, "Emergence and Fundamentality," p. 882.
[18] Barnes, "Emergence and Fundamentality," p. 880.
[19] Barnes, "Emergence and Fundamentality," p. 876.

"An emergent thing is a robust ontological commitment—something new, distinct from the sum of its parts. And so, ostensibly, it is one of the things God would have to create in order to make the world how it is."[20] Furthermore, if evaluative aesthetic qualities are, as I have been suggesting, emergent entities, then they too are *fundamental* entities, "a robust ontological commitment," "things God would have to create in order to make the world how it is." And *that* certainly appears to be *realism* with regard to evaluative aesthetic properties.

But before I close the case for realism with regard to evaluative aesthetic properties let me adduce one further consideration in its favor. In his seminal article on moral realism, Peter Railton made it an essential feature of the doctrine (as he was defending it) "that moral inquiry is of a piece with empirical inquiry."[21] Or, in other words, there is a "science" of morality in the "natural science" sense of that word.

Many find the notion of moral inquiry as scientific inquiry a highly suspect notion, even, it should be remarked, *defenders* of moral realism. Thus Shafer-Landau argues: "As I see it, there are genuine features of our world that remain forever outside the purview of the natural sciences. Moral facts are such features."[22]

But might I suggest that the empirical study of evaluative aesthetic features does not strike one with the prima facie "oddness" that the notion of "moral science" obviously does. Indeed, there are those in well-established sciences—biology, evolutionary biology, neuro-science, and psychology, to name the most prominent—who are doing research in various aspects of the "aesthetic," as they call it, and, publishing their results in reputable venues.

I confess that I am skeptical of many of the "results" of those endeavors with which I am acquainted. To put it baldly, I don't think a lot of the science is very good; and the understanding of the "aesthetic" on the part of those doing the science I find shallow to the point of naivety. *But*—and this is the important point—the prospects don't seem to me to be conceptually absurd, or doomed, ultimately, to failure: in Shafer-Landau's words, "forever outside the purview of the natural sciences."

---

[20] Barnes, "Emergence and Fundamentality," p. 885.

[21] Peter Railton, "Moral Realism," *Philosophical Review*, 95 (1986), p. 165.

[22] Shafer-Landau, *Moral Realism*, p. 4.

We have, after all, evidence of, if I may so put it, an "aesthetic sensibility" in the human animal, as far back as Neanderthal, and perhaps even before. We have the extraordinary cave paintings, of course. But we have artifacts even earlier that seem to have been worked in such a way that we feel compelled to call it "aesthetic." Perhaps I am letting myself be carried away. However, I cannot help thinking that *Homo sapiens* might well be denominated *Homo aestheticus* into the bargain. And if what I have called "aesthetic sensibility" is coeval with being human, then, we might think, it is so deeply embedded in the human fiber as to be in one sense or other a "natural phenomenon," and, therefore, a proper object of natural science. So here may be another way in which aesthetic realism seems less problematic than its moral counterpart. If being susceptible of scientific inquiry is a condition on realism, then aesthetic realism seems, in that regard, the more likely candidate.

But to return now to the notion of evaluative aesthetic properties as emergent entities, the problem of "value" remains unaddressed. It is, of course, one thing to be an emergent entity, and problems enough there. It is yet another thing to be an emergent *value* entity, yet more problems in the offing. The point is, clearly, that someone who has no problem with the notion of emergent entities *simpliciter* may well have a problem with emergent value entities because he or she has a problem with value realism, which the notion of emergent value entities implies.

What then is the prima facie difficulty with value properties as "features of the world"? As Shafer-Landau puts it, with regard to moral realism, what he calls *moral facts* "introduce an element of normativity that cannot be captured by the natural sciences." And he continues: "They tell us what we *ought* to do, how we *should* behave, what is *worthy* of pursuing, what *reasons* we have, what is *justifiable* and what not."[23]

It is noteworthy, but not surprising, how strong the emphasis is, in Shafer-Landau's statement of the problem, on the action-oriented aspect of *normativity*. For, as I have pointed out in previous chapters, it is that very thing, that very orientation, that emotivism and expressivism are so well suited to address. In that respect, though, as I have pointed out in previous chapters, judgments of taste differ from moral judgments in *not* telling us "what we *ought* to do, how we *should* behave." So if part of the

---

[23] Shafer-Landau, *Moral Realism*, p. 4.

problem of "moral facts" is that "They tell us what we *ought* to do, how we *should* behave . . . ," it does not seem as if evaluative aesthetic feature "facts" have that problem. So there is at least a prima facie plus for aesthetic realism vis-à-vis evaluative aesthetic features.

Here ends my defense, such as it is, moderate though it is, of aesthetic realism with regard to evaluative aesthetic features. However, let us remind ourselves yet again that the question is: Why do we dispute over taste? And a proper answer to it, with regard to evaluative aesthetic features, does not require the truth of aesthetic realism, merely the *belief* in it. And that is a far less contentious matter (although, as we shall see, not entirely uncontentious). It is an argument to the best explanation. The art-interested dispute over evaluative aesthetic features of artworks because they believe, correctly or not, that they are disputing over matters of fact.

But of course, although such disputes do at times take place with no *other* end in view than establishing the presence or absence of the evaluative aesthetic features at issue, I suggest, and I dare say it is not an outlandish suggestion, that the ultimate end in view more often than not is some verdict as to the worth of the artwork, the evidence for which is the presence or absence of aesthetic features. In other words, disputes over the presence or absence of aesthetic features in artworks more often than not cash out as disputes, ultimately, over the merit (or lack thereof) of the artworks themselves.

And so we are now left with the question, Why do we dispute over taste? where the subject in dispute is artistic merit. To that question I now turn.

14

The Truth of Evaluation

The art-interested, I claim, dispute often and vigorously, sometimes even *passionately*, about the relative artistic merit of artworks. It seems natural and obvious that they do so. Nor need they be art-experts to do so.

A dentist and an accountant walk out of a local cinema after having viewed a revival of an old Hollywood classic. They then betake themselves to a local watering hole and order drinks. What do they talk about? The chances are, I think, that they don't talk shop. They talk about the movie.

But why a dentist and an accountant? Am I suggesting that members of these professions are philistines? By no means. What I wanted were two well-educated individuals: not however educated to be experts in any one of the arts, but art-interested in at least one of the arts, and competent appreciators in the sense of "competent" discussed previously: Humean competent, as I read Hume. A dentist and an accountant seemed to fit the bill. I am sure my readers can think of others, all members of the vast populous that constitute the non-expert, well-informed, art-interested. That being clarified, I return to my dentist and accountant.

The accountant didn't think much of the movie. The dentist did. And the dentist, quite naturally, tries to convince his friend that the film really was quite successful. Furthermore, he does so by, among other things, pointing out what I have been calling aesthetic features, both the emergent and non-emergent ones, the presence of which in the film he thinks are what makes it a successful one: what makes it a *good movie.*

His friend may disagree with him about the presence of the features in question. So the argument over the merit of the movie may well reduce to an argument over whether the aesthetic features are present and whether they are sufficient to make the movie a good one.

Now the dentist and the accountant, as I imagine them, have no technical knowledge of movie-making technique. They do not know what point-of-view editing is. They do not know that length of shot is an important feature to notice in film analysis. They do not know what soft focus and depth of field are. And so on.

But they know how to talk in ordinary conversational language about the aspects of the film that cause the audiences for which such films are made to appreciate them. And they are not unusual in wanting to talk about the film they have just seen and dispute over its merits or defects in regard to the aesthetic features it may or may not possess.

I have mentioned, so far, only my friends' discussion of the film's aesthetic properties. But if the film they have just seen has any significant depth to it, they may also find themselves talking about its meaning properties. In other words, they have passed on from analysis to interpretation.

And now I recall what film they are discussing. It is that Hollywood masterpiece, the romantic comedy, *The Philadelphia Story*. The plot is what I describe as the wrong-mate right-mate archetype, in which events begin with the hero or heroine on the verge of marrying the wrong mate and, of course, ending up with the right match being made, after numerous shenanigans. *The Philadelphia Story* is complicated in that the wrong-mate right-mate structure is also an example of what Stanley Cavell has identified as the plot of re-marriage. For the story begins with the Katherine Hepburn character divorced from the Cary Grant character and about to marry the wrong mate. She ends up, of course, re-marrying the Cary Grant character, right mate after all, the divorce to the contrary notwithstanding.

Now it may seem perverse to look for anything beyond supreme entertainment value in such a confection as *The Philadelphia Story*, but that I think is too facile a conclusion, and my view is shared by the accountant (who worked his way through school). For in spite of all the palpably engaging comic and aesthetic features the film presents, it seems to the accountant, self-made man that he is, that it left him with an uncomfortable feeling about the view it seems to him to project of the social classes. To put it bluntly, it ennobles the rich, by inheritance, over the ambitious, upwardly mobile middle class.

The villain of the piece is an ambitious character, having worked his way up through the ranks, and about to marry into high society. But it is the rich and privileged that have all the charm, all the culture, and the moral high ground into the bargain. The lower classes consist of either faithful servants or, in the case of the "wrong mate," an over-reaching moral prig.

For all of their charms, the accountant puts it to his friend, that the rich and privileged, and the two initially hostile visitors they "convert" possess, to anyone with moral sensibilities and social conscience, there is a smugness and snobbery about them that make the ending of the movie less morally appealing than was intended.[1]

Thus the argument between the accountant and the dentist over the artistic merit of *The Philadelphia Story* involves *both* analysis *and* interpretation. The dentist touts the very attractive aesthetic features of the film, its setting, its humor, its intriguing characters and amusing plot as his reasons for believing that it is a really great film of its genre, while the accountant points to the moral flaws of the "world view," if that is not too pretentious a description of it, that he sees the movie as projecting, in defense of his negative judgment of its merit.

Now I chose these two personages to make my point here with purposeful intent. They are intelligent, well-educated, and successful men in their chosen professions. But they are, as I see them, at the lower end of the art-interested. They do not frequent art museums except under duress, when vacationing in Paris or London. And they are at the movies together because their wives are at an all-Beethoven concert in Carnegie Hall, a place they do not frequent. But they *are* art-interested. They enjoy movies and, occasionally, plays.

Why are they arguing about *The Philadelphia Story*? If you asked them, I think the dentist and accountant would be nonplussed, would find the question as odd as being asked why they are arguing about any other "matter of fact." I am not suggesting that the two have given any thought whatever to the metaphysical question of what *kind* of "matter of fact" the artistic value or disvalue of *The Philadelphia Story* might be.

---

[1] I have always suspected that Philip Barry, the playwright, intended with *The Philadelphia Story*, to "even things up," so to speak, and present the rich and privileged in a more sympathetic light, in contrast to the way they were portrayed in his previous film, *Holiday*, which also exhibits the wrong mate–right mate plot archetype, but has the hero a self-made man who has worked his way through college, achieved success by virtue of his own labor, and rejects his wealthy prospective father-in-law's domination and offer of quick riches and a preprogrammed life.

Indeed, I would insist, rather, that they are just natural born, unreflective "artistic value realists." And my reason for so insisting is that it is an argument to the best explanation. They are *not* disputing with an end in view of motivating to action. The default explanation is that they are disputing simply about what they take to be a factual matter.

Suppose now we work our way up the ladder of the art-interested from the lower rungs to the higher. What is it reasonable to conjecture we would find vis-à-vis disputation over artistic merit?

Surely it is a reasonable conjecture that the more intensely art-interested one is, the more vigorously, the more passionately one will argue for one's evaluations of works of art. And, of course, it is equally reasonable to conjecture that the more intensely art-interested one is the more technical and historical and critical knowledge one will bring to bear in the dispute. And again: Why do we dispute over taste? And yet again the only explanation that seems available is that the art-sophisticated, no less than accountants and dentists, are, deep down, whether they bring it to consciousness or not, dyed-in-the-wool artistic value realists. They really believe they are disputing about *something*, not merely venting their passions, when they dispute over the merits of artworks and artists.

But, it may be objected, there must certainly be, among the art-interested, those who are *not* artistic value realists. It is surely an exaggeration to claim that art-value realism is the only game in town.

The point is well taken. After all, as Hume pointed out in "Of the Standard of Taste," there seem to be, as he put it, *two* "species" of "common sense," not merely the one that holds Milton's superiority to Ogilby as solid a matter of fact as Tenerife's towering over a molehill, but the one that holds *De gustibus non disputandum est.*[2] Thus one "source," as it were, of the belief, among the art-interested, that artistic merit, or lack thereof, is *not* a matter of fact but a matter of 'taste," or "attitude" (or whatever term you favor for "subjective") is intuition or, as Hume put it, "common sense." And one would assume that no matter how wide-spread this belief in *De gustibus non disputandum est*, it occurs among the less sophisticated of the art-interested: those who have not come to this belief through philosophical or art-theoretical reflection; rather in

---

[2] Hume, "Of the Standard of Taste," *Essays*, p. 235.

the usual, informal and haphazard ways in which our ordinary beliefs and "intuitions" are formed.

However, among the more sophisticated of the art-interested one would, I think, expect those who reject evaluative art realism to have reached this conclusion on the basis of some kind of argument or other. It might be philosophical argument, of which there is a long history from the birth of modern aesthetics in the eighteenth century. Or it might take the form of some sociological or political "deconstruction" of the "myth" of artistic value objectivity: an "explanation" for how we have been brainwashed or conditioned to the belief that Milton is "objectively" better than Ogilby or Beethoven than Anton Reicha.

No convincing argument of any kind to that effect has, I must say, ever crossed my desk. This of course does not prove that none is waiting in the wings or that evaluative art realism is true. But be all that as it may, my question is this. How widespread *is* the belief among the art-interested that evaluative art realism is false; how widespread the belief among the art-interested that *De gustibus non disputandum est*?

In essence it is after all an easy question to answer, requiring no metaphysical depths to plumb. Make a survey! Take a poll! The question is open to uncomplicated methods of empirical enquiry.

But no such inquiry has ever been undertaken, at least so far as I am aware. So let me propose, in lieu of that, the following, alas, inconclusive argument.

I take it that it would be *irrational* for anyone who believed *De gustibus non disputandum est*, with regard to artistic value, either intuitively, or by dint of argument, to engage in a dispute about artistic value, unless, of course, the individual had some ulterior, practical motive for wanting to bring someone round to her positive or negative attitude towards some work of art or other, to motivate appropriate action, for instance. But as I have argued at length, there are few, and unusual instances in which a dispute over artistic value has as its conclusion some action or other. And the operative motive that remains an option for explaining why such disputes occur is convincing one's opponent of *the truth*.

That having been said let me propose the following argument. There is, and has been since classical antiquity, widespread, vigorous, many times even passionate dispute about the value, disvalue, and comparative value of artworks. If one believes that matters of artistic value are purely subjective, and not matters of fact, then it would be irrational for one to engage in disputation over artistic value, disvalue or comparative value. However, if the belief that matters of artistic value are purely subjective and not matters of fact *were* widespread among the art-interested, then we would have to conclude that in this regard the majority of the art-interested have been and are deeply irrational. But it seems preposterous to thank that irrationality in this regard predominates among the art-interested. So it seems reasonable to conclude that in this regard the art-interested are more or less *rational*, and that, therefore, they are predominantly realists with regard to artistic value, disvalue, and comparative value.

Now I am not for a moment claiming that irrationality is not alive and well, walking to and fro in the world. What I am claiming in the above argument is merely that there is no reason to believe that it is especially rampant among the art-interested. Thus, if we assume the art-interested are no less rational than the rest of humanity, then we must assume that they act rationally when they engage in dispute over artistic value. And if they were not realists of some stripe, with regard to artistic value, they would be acting irrationally in so disputing. The conclusion that seems to press itself upon us then is that by and large the art-interested are art value realists. It is the only plausible explanation for their behavior that can acquit them of the charge of *irrationality*.

Furthermore, we can safely conclude that the explanation for why the art-interested dispute over art value is the widespread belief among them in art value realism. Given this belief, their behavior is altogether rational. But is the *belief* rational? Which is to say, are there any rational grounds for believing that art value realism is *true*?

As in the case of disputes over art meaning and disputes over the aesthetic features of artworks, the explanation for why we dispute over taste goes through whether or not the belief in realism anent the respective properties is true or not. All that is necessary is that the belief be in place.

But again, as with artistic meaning realism and aesthetic feature realism, I want at least to explore the question of whether art value realism has any legs. And again, as in the previous two cases, a thorough exploration is beyond the purview of the present project. So I propose to explore a single argument that tends to support artistic value realism. I shall call it the Convergence Argument.

Let me begin by going back yet again to the eighteenth century and to Hume. An informal argument that frequently has surfaced in the philosophical literature as well as in ordinary conversation is what might be called the Non-Convergence Argument, or perhaps the Argument to Disagreement. It begins with the assertion that there is well-neigh universal disagreement over matters of artistic taste. As Hume puts the point, in "Of the Standard of Taste," "As this variety of taste is obvious to the most careless inquirer, so will it be found, on examination, to be still greater in reality than in appearance."[3]

So, the argument goes, if art value realism were true, if it really were a matter of fact that this artwork or that is great or mediocre compared to that one, there would emerge, in the long run, at least, general agreement. For in matters of fact, be it scientific fact, or the ordinary facts of ordinary life, opinion tends to converge; agreement is achieved; consensus emerges. But that does not happen in matters of taste in the arts. Rather, dissention reigns. "As this variety of taste is obvious to the most careless inquirer, so will it be found on examination, to be still greater in reality than in appearance." Surely this clear lack of convergence, this absence of eventual convergence upon "the truth" in matters of taste in art strongly suggests that it is not facts that are at stake here but that we are in the realm of pure personal preference. Such, in brief, is the Argument to Disagreement, the Non-Convergence Argument.

However, interestingly enough, Hume seems, towards the close of the essay on taste, to back away from his initial observations on the great variety of taste in the arts, and to perceive, in the end, more consensus than disagreement. "The same Homer who pleased at Athens and Rome two thousand years ago, is still admired in Paris and London." And further: "It appears, then, that amidst all the variety and caprice of taste, there are certain general principles of approbation or blame, whose influence a careful eye may trace in all operations of the mind."[4]

In the first of the passages just quoted—I will get to the second by and by—Hume is, of course, alluding to what has been called "the test of time," and, obliquely, to what is often termed, in many of the various arts, "the canon." And what the test of time and the canon seem to

---

[3] Hume, "Of the Standard of Taste," *Essays*, p. 231.
[4] Hume, "Of the Standard of Taste," *Essays*, pp. 237–8.

strongly suggest is that the Argument to Disagreement to the contrary notwithstanding, there *is* a tendency towards consensus in art evaluation. If there were not, the test of time wouldn't produce a canon.

The consensus that the canon represents might be taken to support art value realism in at least two ways. One might argue that the best explanation for the existence of the canon, for the consensus of opinion concerning the value of artworks is that the value or disvalue or comparative value of artworks is a matter of fact. Or, one might present a weaker argument to the effect that the existence of the canon at least defuses one argument *against* art value realism, namely, the Argument to Disagreement, which says that the lack of consensus on art value is incompatible with art value realism.

Now to the stronger claim, that the argument to the best explanation for the consensus the canon represents is art value realism, the skeptical might well reply in this wise. There are other explanations available for the existence of the canon, and the consensus it implies, that avoid the ontological difficulties of art value realism. All of them involve some kind of ideological, political, or socio-economic "conditioning" that produces consensus. I will not go into chapter and verse about the matter. All of my readers will be familiar with such explanations, in one form or another. And I do not know of a single one that holds water, as I have previously said. But perhaps a further word is in order before I go on.

I am, needless to say, not unaware of the controversy that surrounds the canon, as I have indicated above, in particular the charge that it is merely an elitist construction, and does not reflect a genuine consensus with regard to real artistic value. The foremost source, perhaps, of this, what might be termed, ideological deconstruction, is the well-known claim that the canon simply results from the preferences of the well-to-do over the working class. The art of the canon, so it is said, is the expensive art.

I shall not try to defend the canon against this charge, and others like it here, as I have indicated above. What I do want merely to point out is that the ball is in the deconstructionists' court. The canon, the consensus *exists*. And there is no gainsaying that. Furthermore, the consensus the canon represents has as its most obvious, prima facie explanation, that over the course of time, under continued scrutiny, those works that have joined the canon have done so because this continued scrutiny has discovered in them real value-making features.

This *may* be a put-up job, as the elitist argument claims. The canon may represent nothing more than the preferences of the ruling class. Although the elitist argument must tell us *what* it is in art that causes the ruling class to elevate this work of art into the canon rather than that. But in any case, it appears to me that the burden of proof is on the elitist theorist to *show* that the prima facie explanation for the consensus and the canon is false and the elitist theory true. And as I remarked above, I have never encountered an elitist argument to that effect that holds water; and until I do, I will hew to the prima facie explanation, which I believe to be the man on the street's explanation as well, that the test of time converges on a consensus as to the value of artworks, and this elevates them into what we know as the canon.

However, a word more is in order about the test of time itself. Hume indeed was alluding to it when he observed, as I quoted him above, that "The same Homer who pleased in Athens and Rome two thousand years ago, is still admired in Paris and London." And, as he continued his thought: "All the changes of climate, government, religion, and language, have not been able to obscure his glory." But Hume also was aware, however, that the test of time is not an unbroken continuity in which what is valued at its creation is valued forever, and what is disvalued at its creation is disvalued forever. For, as he further observes: "Authority or prejudice may give a temporary vogue to a bad poet or orator; but his reputation will never be durable or general." Whereas "a real genius, the longer his works endure, and the more wide they are spread, the more sincere is the admiration which he meets with."[5]

Nor should we overlook, as Hume apparently does, the other side of the coin: the genius, not as valued in his time as his lesser contemporaries, whom the test of time ultimately elevates into the canon. Telemann, it will be recalled, *not* Bach, was Leipzig's first choice for Cantor at the *Thomaskirche*. Or, to instance another well-known case in point, Mozart's *La Clemenza di Tito* was described by a distinguished member of its first audience as "German trash."

Surely, though, that the test of time in the arts exhibits complications, and the path to consensus sometimes straight, but frequently crooked, hardly are reasons for rejecting it. For if they were, scientific consensus

---

[5] Hume, "Of the Standard of Taste," *Essays*, pp. 237–8.

would suffer the same fate, witness, for example, the complex history of the wave theory versus the corpuscular theory of light. So far, the test of time, on my view, has survived the test of time.

I shall put up no further defense of the validity of the canon or the consensus it represents here against the charges discussed just now. But one thing is clear. There is a tendency among all of the above-named deflationary "explanations" of the canon to *assume* from the get-go that artistic value is "a matter of taste"; to *assume* from the get-go that art value realism is a non-starter and that, therefore, the canon is to be explained by the influence of custom, economics, politics, social conditioning, and the like. However, *De gustibus non disputandum est* requires argument. That it is a common saying does not suffice, for, as Hume observed, it is not the only intuition in town. And the existence of the canon puts paid to the Non-Consensus Argument, which is usually thought by the "subjectivists" as sufficient to establish their view.

Now perhaps at this point the "subjectivist" may dig in his heels and argue that, well, "There is 'consensus' and there is *consensus*." To be sure, there is consensus as to who and what belong in the literary or musical or fine-arts canon, more or less. But it is not firm, solid, universal consensus that the sciences produce.

But I believe that claim to be false. And here is why. Needless to say, no matter how firmly entrenched an artist or artwork is in the canon, a distinguished dissenter can always be found. However, it is my experience, limited albeit that it is, that the very same can be said for many of the widely accepted theories and conclusions in both the soft and hard sciences.

I am a regular reader of *Science News*, a periodical devoted to the dissemination of cutting edge scientific research to the laity. And it doesn't take long to catch on to the formula that almost every article therein cleaves to. The dénouement is as predictable as the final scene in a detective movie, with all of the suspects present and Nick Charles about to reveal "whodunit."

Here, for example, is how it goes. Recent observational data, and new computer models making use of it, have led to a theory of planet formation proposed by Professor X of MIT, and published by the prestigious scientific journal *Nature*. After the theory is explained, in layman's terms, by one of the *Science News'* popular science writers, she then quotes five or so other equally prestigious planetary scientists who applaud the theory as a significant breakthrough and unqualifiedly endorse it. But inevitably such an article ends, obviously for "dramatic" effect, with a dissenting voice, equally prestigious, with a different interpretation of the data, who rejects the conclusion. There is, in other words, ever and again, someone to hang the scientific jury.

Notice that the dissenters are not kooks or crazies. This is not a matter of the Flat Earth Society or Foundational Creationism. It emanates from authorities as eminent and professionally well qualified as those who constitute the (more or less) consensus.

Thus what I am claiming is that although there may be less, there is not significantly less consensus over the canon, over artistic value, than there is over most (I will not say all) of the conclusions of the natural sciences. Nor is there significantly more dissension. As Hume puts it for dissension over artistic value, which might apply, with suitable adjustment of terms, for scientific dissension: "But where there is such a diversity in the internal frame or external situation as is entirely blameless on both sides, and leaves no room to give one the preference above the other; in that case a certain degree of diversity in judgement is unavoidable."[6]

This having been said, I want to return, as I promised I would, to the quotation from Hume, that bolsters his claim for the artistic value consensus, which goes, you will recall: "It appears, then, that amidst all the variety of taste, there are certain general principles of appreciation or blame, whose influence a careful eye may trace in all operations of the mind."

How are these "general principles of appreciation or blame" to be discovered? Not surprisingly, in the Humean manner, which is to say, through *experience*. "It is evident," Hume writes, "that none of the rules of composition are fixed by reasonings a priori, or can be esteemed abstract conclusions of the understanding, from comparing those habitudes and relations of ideas, which are eternal and immutable. Their foundation," he continues, "is the same with that of all the *practical sciences*, experience; nor are they any thing but general observations, concerning what has been universally found to please in all countries and in all ages."[7]

Needless to say, the term "science" had not yet attained the meaning it has for us, in Hume's day, "natural philosophy" being still the term of

---

[6] Hume, "Of the Standard of Taste," *Essays*, p. 250.

[7] Hume, "Of the Standard of Taste," *Essays*, pp. 235–6. Italics mine.

choice. So I presume Hume had in mind by "practical sciences" what we would describe as "crafts," and practical skills, rather than "applied sciences." Be that as it may, it *is* highly suggestive in Hume's account that artistic value consensus should be seen by Hume as the result of "science," in the sense, at least, of a systematic inquiry founded upon "experience," which is to say, Humean *induction*, common as well to what he knew as natural philosophy and we as natural science.

And, interestingly enough, a more recent philosopher than David Hume has argued that there are scientific explanatory reasons for believing in what he terms the *Thesis of Rationality in Aesthetics*.[8] The philosopher I have reference to is Michael A. Slote, whose article of 1971, "The Rationality of Aesthetic Value Judgments," seems to me to deserve more attention from philosophers of art than it has ever received. I shall conclude this chapter with a discussion of some points in Slote's article relevant to present concerns.

Slote, like Hume, initiates his argument with what I take to be the perception of more or less general art value consensus. He begins: "In all the arts with which I am acquainted—music, drama, poetry, etc.— there exists a certain long-term unidirectionality with respect to changes in certain kinds of aesthetic preferences."[9] Thus, for example (and it is Slote's favorite example): "Almost everyone who spends a good deal of time listening to music tends to prefer the music of Mozart to that of Bruckner."[10] But, furthermore, and crucially, "the longer people are exposed to the music of these composers and to music in general and the more they learn about the purely technical aspects of music, the more there are who come to prefer Mozart, if they haven't liked Mozart better from the start...The flow of musical appreciation and liking is from Bruckner to Mozart in general."[11] And this phenomenon, Slote claims, can be generalized for all of the arts, which is to say, "long term unidirectionality...with respect to other pairs of artists or works of art."[12]

---

[8] Michael A. Slote, "The Rationality of Aesthetic Value Judgments," *The Journal of Philosophy*, 68 (1971), p. 821.

[9] Slote, "The Rationality of Aesthetic Value Judgments," p. 822.

[10] Slote, "The Rationality of Aesthetic Value Judgments," p. 822.

[11] Slote, "The Rationality of Aesthetic Value Judgments," p. 823.

[12] Slote, "The Rationality of Aesthetic Value Judgments," p. 823.

Like Hume as well, Slote recognizes that although artistic value judgments tend to converge on consensus, inevitable disagreement will remain. As Slote puts this point, again with a musical example: "There are some pairs of composers such that many people prefer a given one of them to the other, at the same time that many other people have just the opposite preference. A good example of this might be the composers Brahms and Wagner . . . There thus seems to be *no* unidirectionality of preference change with respect to the music of Brahms and Wagner."[13]

What seems to me particularly noteworthy here is that Slote's characterization of the tendency towards consensus in artistic value judgment—the "unidirectionality," as he calls it—and, as well, his characterization of the cases of persistent, irreconcilable disagreement, are almost a carbon copy of Hume's characterization of the same phenomena. And, significantly, there is no evidence that Slote was acquainted with Hume's essay on taste. (Few philosophers *were* in 1971.)

Thus both Hume and Slote see consensus where the objects of artistic value judgments are wide apart: Milton versus Ogilby, in Hume's account, Mozart versus Bruckner in Slote's (although Bruckner, of course, *is* in the canon, whereas Ogilby, clearly, is not). Similarly, both Hume and Slote see irreconcilable difference in evaluation where the objects of artistic value judgment are of outstanding merit: Ovid versus Horace versus Tacitus, in Hume's account,[14] Brahms versus Wagner in Slote's.

My point here is that two distinguished philosophers, one in the eighteenth century, one in the twentieth, separated by some 250 years, both surveying the art scenes of their respective times, come to the same conclusion: that there is a tendency towards convergence, towards consensus in artistic value judgments. Of course two philosophers can agree and both be wrong. But surely the existence of the canon, in all of the arts, is something that one hardly requires philosophy to descry. So I will take that as settled.

But, furthermore, Slote, like Hume, envisions the possibility of an explanation, on inductive grounds, of convergence in artistic value judgment. And in Slote's case, the explanation envisioned seems "scientific," in the modern, robust sense of the term. Slote writes: "That there is

---

13 Slote, "The Rationality of Aesthetic Value Judgments," p. 822.
14 Hume, "Of the Standard of Taste," *Essays*, p. 250.

such an unidirectionality in various of the arts seems an interesting fact. And it is a fact that calls for explanation."[15] What sort of explanation could that be?

According to Slote: "If one says of someone who dies that his death was caused by something entering his heart, what one said is very general and fairly uninformative; but one has at least ruled out *certain* causes of death ... so that what one says has some sort of explanatory function. So," Slote goes on, "I am inclined to treat the above as some sort of (vague) explanation of a man's death and to treat the claim that Mozart-Bruckner unidirectionality is due to some sort of physiological-cum psychological mechanism (as well as to the character of Mozart's and Bruckner's music) as a very general and unspecific sort of explanation as well."[16]

Of course Slote's "scientific" explanation, like Hume's, for the artistic value consensus, for the canon, is more of a promissory note than money in the bank. But that does not concern me. For my claim here is not that we have anything like a real worked out science of artistic value. Rather, it is the far less ambitious claim merely that the idea of such a scientific explanation for the artistic value consensus is not "off the wall." And that I think is what one can at least minimally conclude from a reading of Slote's insightful article.

Does Slote's view amount to a form of artistic value realism? Without exploring the details of his article, which are numerous and suggestive, I will quote what I take to be his general conclusion with regard to what I have been calling "artistic value," and what Slote refers to, more generally, as "aesthetic value properties," although it is clear that art is what Slote principally has in mind. He writes: "I believe that many aesthetic (and other) value properties are dispositional properties, and that many aesthetic (and other) value terms have much the same sort of meaning as such scientific and common-sense dispositional terms as 'soluble,' 'brittle,' 'magnetic,' and 'flexible.'"[17]

Is this artistic value "realism"? Well, "soluble," "brittle," "magnetic," "flexible," and other such scientific and common sense dispositional properties are *real* enough for my money, although I am not saying

[15] Slote, "The Rationality of Aesthetic Value Judgments," p. 823.
[16] Slote, "The Rationality of Aesthetic Value Judgments," p. 827.
[17] Slote, "The Rationality of Aesthetic Value Judgments," p. 834.

that I buy into the dispositional property model. But in any event, my purpose, as I have said before, is not to argue for artistic value realism, merely to explore its plausibility or at least its possibility. And my main point, again as I have said before, is that explaining why we dispute over taste, with regard to artistic value, which is the purpose of the present chapter, does not require establishing the truth of artistic value realism, merely establishing that the art-interested are, at heart, artistic value realists; for that alone explains why they dispute over artistic value, whether or not their belief, explicit or inexplicit, conscious or unconscious, in artistic value realism is true.

But at this point a final question arises. Needless to say, there *are* those among the art-interested who are *not* art value realists; who are rather, either sophisticated philosophical skeptics, who espouse some form of "expressiveness," and, perhaps, an "error theory" of artistic value into the bargain, or those who, as Hume would put it, subscribe, explicitly or implicitly, consciously or unconsciously, to the first species of common sense, which has it that *De gustibus non disputandum est.*

Do *such* folks dispute over artistic value? If they do, does that knock my explanation of why folks dispute over taste into a cocked hat? To these questions I now turn in the next, and concluding chapter of this monograph.

15

Common Sense and the Error Theory

Why is there disputing over taste? I have ventured to suggest in considering this question on these pages that, for one thing, philosophers of art (and, for that matter, philosophers in general) have paid little attention to it, and that it requires answering.

Frequently in the past, not surprisingly, aesthetic and artistic value judgments have been compared with moral judgments of the right and the good. Some have argued that whereas moral judgments have some rational or objective basis, aesthetic and artistic value judgments do not. Those who have made such an argument have either concluded, falsely, that we do not argue for or against aesthetic and artistic value judgments, or else they have simply failed to raise or attempt to answer the question of *why* we patently *do* dispute over such matters.

On the other hand, there have been those who put both moral judgments and judgments of aesthetic and artistic value down as in some sense or other "mere" expressions of attitude, with no claim to be stating matters of "fact," since, on these views, there cannot be such things in the world as value facts: values *in* the world. And although, as I argued above, such "attitude" or "expressionist" theorists have no difficulty accounting for why we should engage in moral disputes, they seem to provide no basis for explaining why we should dispute over matters of aesthetic and artistic value, which manifestly we *do*. For moral disputation, which is to say, practical reasoning, has as its goal, usually (but not by any means always) motivation to action, whereas aesthetic and artistic disputation over value seldom do. Why, then, argue over taste?

My answer to this question, it will be recalled, was twofold. First, I suggested that the two basic reasons for trying to convince the "other" that you are "right" and he or she "wrong" is to get the other to do or not do something; or, simply, to convince the other that you are in possession of the truth about something, you are in possession of "the facts," and the other is not. And, second, I suggested that since motivation to action is seldom the reason for convincing the other that you are "right" and he or she "wrong," in a matter of taste, of aesthetic or artistic value or meaning, the remaining reason must clearly be the operative one. The art-interested are, basically, realists about meaning in the arts, and about aesthetic and artistic value. They think these matters are matters of truth or falsity: matters of fact. And that is reason enough for one to argue with and try to convince the other in these matters.

But I now, in the present chapter, want to consider two anomalous characters, if you will, among the art-interested. The first adheres to what Hume called the species of common sense which has it that *De gustibus non disputandum est*. But, *in spite of that*, this character argues about taste nevertheless. That is what makes him or her anomalous. For it is clearly irrational to argue over matters of taste if you adhere to Hume's species of common sense which endorses *De gustibus non disputandum est*.

The second character is more complicated. This character is an adherent to what is known in philosophical circles as the "error theory" of value. For if one believes either the error theory of value, *tout court*, or merely the error theory of aesthetic and artistic value, then it would be irrational for such a person to engage in disputation over aesthetic or artistic value. So my second anomalous character among the art-interested, if there is such a character, comes in two varieties: what I shall call the "total error theorist," whose skepticism extends to all forms of value; and the "limited error theorist," whose skepticism extends only to aesthetic and artistic value.

I shall characterize the error theory in more detail later on. But I want first to deal with the character who adheres to Hume's first species of common sense, namely, *De gustibus non disputandum est*, yet, nevertheless, engages in disputes over taste in art and the aesthetic.

Is there such an anomalous character as this? On the assumption that almost anything, no matter how weird, is possible, I will assume that there is, although how widespread the eccentricity may be among the art-interested I will not venture to guess. I shall call this individual the Humean character. Here is how I picture him.

The Humean character belongs, of course, to the art-interested. And he subscribes to Hume's first species of common sense. But it *is* common sense, not some carefully worked out value-skepticism that the Humean character has as the basis of his belief that there is no disputing over taste. Of course behind his value-skepticism is some informal set of reasons. Perhaps he is in thrall to the belief that the assumed wide irreconcilable variety of taste in art belies any notion of an "objective" standard of taste. Or perhaps he has some vague notion of the fact-value distinction driving his skepticism.

In any case, when asked, his view is *De gustibus non disputandum est*. Yet, when he reads a novel or sees a movie that he very much enjoys, and that his friend does not, he is taken aback, and *De gustibus non disputandum est* to the contrary notwithstanding, he launches into what seems for all intents and purposes an attempt to convince his friend that he is right about the novel or movie, and his friend is wrong.

Does this sometimes happen? I certainly think it does. Clearly it is a case of all-too-common human irrationality. And perhaps that is all that can be said about it. But let me try to say a little bit more about it by way of anecdote. I do not recall its source. But here it is.

Parmenides and Zeno are at a horse race. As the race proceeds, Zeno gets so caught up in the excitement that he shouts: "Run, Buceph! Run!" But Parmenides keeps his head, turns to Zeno, and chides: "You know, of course, that this is impossible."

The moral, clearly, of this little fable is that when theory conflicts with ordinary, down-to-earth perception, the latter bubbles to the surface and takes over, unbidden and unwilled. Parmenides' universe is a plenum: in it there is no empty space, and thus there can be no motion, for motion requires space *into* which matter can move. As a consequence, cosmic gridlock prevails, motion an illusion. Furthermore, as Parmenides perhaps is reminding his companion, Zeno himself has "shown" that Buceph cannot possibly win the race, for if he is in the lead, he cannot ever reach the finish line, since to do so would require traversing an infinite number of points, which is impossible in a finite time. And if he is behind, he cannot ever catch up with the horse in the lead because at any point he reaches, the horse in the lead will be a little bit ahead of him, no matter how fast Buceph runs. It is, in other words, a case of the tortoise and the hare.

But Parmenidian theory to the contrary notwithstanding, Zeno cannot help seeing the horse race as anyone else would see it. And so overcome by the illusion of motion, he urges on his favorite, theory forgotten.

The Humean character is, I suggest, in a similar position to Zeno's. He has a "theory," albeit, unlike Zeno's, an informal, more or less intuitive one, not a closely argued philosophical position. But *his* "theory," again to the contrary notwithstanding, confronts the perfectly ordinary phenomenon of a novel or movie, enjoyed by him, not by his friend, and seems powerless against his deep-seated feeling of discomfort that there should be such a disparity in *this* kind of human preference. "How could he *not* have liked it when I liked it so much?" Hume observed that "The principle of natural equality of taste is . . . ," at times, "totally forgot; and while we admit it on some occasions, where the objects seem near an equality, it appears an extravagant paradox, or rather a palpable absurdity, where objects so disproportionate [as Ogilby and Milton] are compared together."[1] But I do not think it is only where objects so disproportionate are compared together that "the natural equality of taste . . . is totally forgot." I think it can be forgot, in perfectly ordinary circumstances, by the Humean character, when confronted by diversity of taste. For all of his insistence, in moments of quasi-philosophical reflection, that "each to his own taste," when confronted with the simple fact of his liking and his friend's disliking of a novel or movie, some sort of basic discomfort kicks in to motivate argument. "Run, Buceph! Run!" he shouts into the wind, while stoutly denying the hare can ever catch the tortoise or the arrow reach the target.

Well, for all of that, I think the Humean character *is* an *anomalous character*, which is to say, a *rare* character, whose *rare* eccentricity manifests itself in a particular form of *irrationality*: believing *De gustibus non disputandum est* while continuing to argue over taste. And, as I have argued above, to single out the art-interested, above all others, as irrational to a man, seems wildly unjustified. So I will leave the Humean character, along with Zeno at the racetrack, as an interesting but untroubling anomaly.

I wish now, however, to move on to what I take to be a more philosophically interesting anomaly, the believer, on philosophical grounds, of the error theory of normative properties, who continues to argue about aesthetic and artistic value. And I will be using as the basis for my discussion a recent article on error theory which proposes the

---

[1] Hume, "Of the Standard of Taste," *Essays*, p. 235.

intriguing thesis that: *we cannot believe the error theory; there is no reason to believe the error theory; and the error theory is true.*[2]

The error theory, as Bart Streumer states it, in his article "Can We Believe the Error Theory?" is as follows: "normative judgments are beliefs that ascribe normative properties, even though such properties do not exist." And he adds: "This theory is normally only defended about moral judgments, but I have argued elsewhere that it seems to be true of all normative judgments."[3] Thus, presumably, on the error theory, when someone (who does not believe the error theory) makes (say) a moral judgment he ascribes a normative property to someone or to some state of affairs, in error, of course, since normative properties, of which moral properties are a sub-set, do not exist, according to the error theory.

But a seeming paradox results if one construes the error theory as pertaining to *all* normative properties. Thus:

The property of being a reason for belief in the sense of a consideration that counts in favor of a belief is a normative property. If the error theory is true, this property does not exist. The error theory therefore entails that there is no reason to believe the error theory.[4]

Furthermore, "we cannot have a belief while believing that there is no reason for this belief."[5] And since the error theory entails that there is no reason to believe the error theory, we cannot believe the error theory, since we cannot believe what we believe there is no reason for believing. However, and here is the seeming paradox, Professor Streumer *defends* the error theory, for: "Just as a theory can be true if we do not believe it, a theory can also be true if we cannot believe it."[6]

Now Professor Streumer, in his very closely argued article, jumps through a lot of logical hoops, and heaps complication upon complication. But much of this would be irrelevant to present concerns, and I will therefore confine myself to what *is* germane.

How can one *both* defend the error theory and yet hold that there is no reason to believe the error theory and (therefore) the error theory cannot

---

[2] Bart Streumer, "Can We Believe the Error Theory?" *The Journal of Philosophy*, 110 (2013).

[3] Streumer, "Can We Believe the Error Theory?" p. 194.

[4] Streumer, "Can We Believe the Error Theory?" p. 197.

[5] Streumer, "Can We Believe the Error Theory?" p. 196.

[6] Streumer, "Can We Believe the Error Theory?" p. 201.

be believed? It seems as if in doing so one is asserting that "The error theory is true but I do not believe it is true" and "The error theory is true but there is no reason for me to believe that it is true," which are both instances of what is sometimes called Moore's paradox: asserting, "p, but I do not believe that p."[7]

Without, as I say, jumping through Streumer's many logical hoops, we can rush on to his general answer to the charge that he has fallen prey to Moore's paradox. Thus he writes: "But I think we can defend the error theory without asserting either of these claims. We can instead assert different parts of the error theory at different times, and assert that there are sound reasons that together seem to show the error theory is true."[8]

We are now in a position to consider my second anomalous character, whom I shall call the "error theory character." He comes in a number of varieties. He might adhere to a moderate version of the error theory that does not apply to reasons for belief; that does not construe reasons for belief as normative properties, but does apply to aesthetic and artistic value properties. (Whether or not he thinks it applies to moral properties is immaterial to my concerns.) Or he could go whole hog and adhere to an error theory that applies to reasons for belief as well.

But in either case the error theory character presents some problems. He continues to argue about taste; he continues to argue about aesthetic and artistic value, even though, according to the error theory, to which he is an adherent, there is nothing to argue about, no truth of the matter, and, as we have seen, there is no other reason he could have for arguing about taste, for arguing about aesthetic and artistic value, if truth were not the issue. His behavior seems entirely incoherent. He is, indeed, an anomaly. What's in it for him?

I think we can venture at least a partial answer to that question, and at least partially explain the error theory character's behavior, by considering an objection to the error theory and Professor Streumer's response to it.

Essentially, Professor Streumer's view, as I have outlined it above, is that the error theorist cannot fully, but only partially believe the error theory. But even "Such partial belief in the error theory," so the objection goes, "will lower our confidence in our normative judgments. It is

[7] Streumer, "Can We Believe the Error Theory?" pp. 210–11.

[8] Streumer, "Can We Believe the Error Theory?" p. 211.

therefore a threat to our normative judgments, including our deepest and most important moral convictions."[9]

Streumer responds: "Though such weak partial belief in the error theory may lower our confidence in our judgments, it will not make us give up these judgments. It is, therefore, no threat to our deepest and most important moral convictions." And he adds, significantly for our purposes, with regard to partial belief in the error theory: "Moreover, it will not affect *which* normative judgments we make, since it will lower our confidence in all possible normative judgments to the same extent."[10]

It seems reasonable to assume that our deepest and most important normative judgments will be the most resistant to belief in the error theory's lowering our confidence in them. And of course *moral* judgments will be among the most obvious and uncontroversial examples of our deepest and most important normative judgments. We therefore have a pretty convincing explanation for why those adhering to the error theory would continue to dispute over matters of morals. Since judgments concerning such matters are some of our deepest and most important normative judgments, weak partial belief in the error theory, as Streumer describes it, will not lower our confidence in such normative judgments. Hence we will continue to argue over them as if they were matters of fact (as well, of course, to influence the *actions* of others, as has been repeatedly pointed out).

But what about aesthetic and artistic value judgments? How will *they* fair with those who hold a weak partial belief in the error theory?

Well, as Streumer claims, weak, partial belief in the error theory "will not affect *which* normative judgments we make, since it will lower our confidence in all possible normative judgments to the same extent." So aesthetic and artistic value judgments are not ruled out from the get-go as possibly being normative judgments that our confidence in will be substantially lowered if we are weak, partial believers in the error theory. If they are some of our deepest and most important normative judgments, then weak, partial belief in the error theory will not be a threat to them. So the question is, are our aesthetic and artistic value judgments some of our deepest and most important normative commitments?

---

[9] Streumer, "Can We Believe the Error Theory?" p. 210.
[10] Streumer, "Can We Believe the Error Theory?" p. 210.

Well, I think we can agree straightaway that normative convictions about aesthetic and artistic value are not as widespread as our moral convictions. For there are few people without moral convictions and considerable numbers of people, I would conjecture, without normative convictions about the artistic and the aesthetic, since such matters simply do not concern them. But, it will be recalled, we already acknowledged this fact and therefore have confined our attention on these pages to what I have described as the "art-interested."

So our question now becomes, are there, among the art-interested, normative convictions concerning art and the aesthetic that are some of our deepest and most important normative convictions? And I venture to suggest that the history of art and the aesthetic gives a resounding "Yes." But that "Yes," needless to say, does not imply that there is any doubt over which the generality of mankind would choose, if it were between rescuing a child or rescuing a Rembrandt from a burning building.

That being settled, let us return to the error theory character who argues over aesthetic and artistic value. Surely he is a *rara avis*; more rare, I dare say, than the Humean character. But I am certain there must be some of his breed, no matter how few, among the art-interested. And we now have a way of dealing with him, given Streumer's position on error theory: a way to explain his propensity for arguing over matters of aesthetic and artistic value, his belief in the error theory *apparently* to the contrary notwithstanding.

Now on Streumer's version of the error theory and its adherent, the error theory character has a weak partial belief in the error theory which lowers his confidence in his aesthetic and artistic value judgments but does *not* force him to give them up. But if he does not give them up, merely has lower confidence in them than those who do not adhere to the error theory, then he must, it would seem, be a realist with regard to aesthetic and artistic value when he is arguing about them, even though his confidence in the truth of aesthetic and artistic value realism is lower than that of the rest of the art-interested. So in effect, our explanation for why the art-interested error theory characters argue over matters of taste is the same as our explanation for why ordinary art-interested citizens do. They are realists with regard to aesthetic and artistic value, albeit realists with doubts.

But now let us remind ourselves that both the Humean character and the error theory character *are* anomalies. They are of the species *rara avis*. So the existence of neither casts doubt on the major thesis of this monograph, namely: the inference to the best explanation for why we dispute over taste is that the art-interested are, implicitly or explicitly, realists with regard to aesthetic and artistic properties.

Whether aesthetic realism and art realism are *true*, I have argued, is irrelevant. The explanation depends only on our *belief*. But it has been an accompanying thesis of this monograph that realism with regard to the meaning properties of art, the aesthetic properties of art, and the value properties of art may be a more plausible position than value theorists, even those that are moral realists, are prepared to allow.

However, as I have stated before, the truth of realism with regard to those properties of artworks that are value properties is a topic for another book; perhaps, indeed, another life. And that is where I will have to leave that question.

I hope what I have succeeded in doing, in the present pages, is to draw the attention of philosophers of art to a phenomenon, namely aesthetic and artistic disputation, which they seem, for the most part, to have taken for granted as unmysterious and, therefore, in no need of exploration or explanation. I hope to have provided at least a beginning for both. Why do we dispute over taste? I hope I have given at least a plausible answer. But in any case, *we do dispute over taste*. That's a fact.

And that leads to a concluding note. As a recent writer has put the problem of moral error theory, its adherents "need to explain why we constantly form moral judgments (rather than refrain from doing so), when their content is such that they imply the existence of something (absolute moral facts) that does not exist."[11] And the same question can be put to the aesthetic and artistic error theorists. I know of no explanation. Of course that we know of no such explanation does not prove that aesthetic and artistic value realism is true. But it may give us pause. If there *are*, out there, aesthetic and artistic *value facts*, they are strange facts indeed. However, as has been said:

> There are more things in heaven and earth,
> Horatio, than are dreamt of in your philosophy.

And perhaps in our philosophy as well.

---

[11] Ragnar Francén Olinder, "Moral Relativism, Error Theory, and Ascriptions of Mistakes," *The Journal of Philosophy*, 110 (2013), p. 579.

Bibliography

Ayer, A. J. *Language, Truth and Logic*. New York: Dover Publications, n.d.

Balguy, John. *A Collection of Tracts Moral and Theological*. London, 1734.

Barnes, Elizabeth. "Emergence and Fundamentality." *Mind*, 121 (2012).

Bearsdley, Monroe C. *The Possibility of Criticism*. Detroit: Wayne State University Press, 1976.

Björnsson, Gunnar, and McPherson, Tristram, "Moral Attitudes for Non-Cognitivists: Solving the Specification Problem." *Mind*, 123 (2014).

Carritt, E. F. "Moral Positivism and Moral Aestheticism." *Philosophy*, 13 (1938).

Carroll, Lewis. *The Complete Works of Lewis Carroll*. Edited by Alexander Woolcott. New York: The Modern Library, n.d.

Debes, Remy. "Recasting Scottish Sentimentalism: The Peculiarity of Moral Approval," *Journal of Scottish Philosophy*, 10 (2012).

Einstein, Alfred. *Gluck*. Translated by Eric Blom. London: J. M. Dent; New York: E. P. Dutton, 1954.

Fish, Stanley. *Is There a Text in This Class? The Authority of Interpretive Communities*. Cambridge, MA: Harvard University Press, 1988.

Goldman, Alan H. *Philosophy and the Novel*. Oxford: Oxford University Press, 2013.

Grice, Paul. *Studies in the Way of Words*. Cambridge, MA, and London: Harvard University Press, 1989.

Hahn, L. E. (ed.). *The Philosophy of A. J. Ayer*. LaSalle, IL: Open Court, 1992.

Hieronymi, Pamela. "Reasons for Action." *Proceedings of the Aristotelian Society*, New Series 111 (1911).

Hirsch, E. D. *Validity in Interpretation*. New Haven and London: Yale University Press, 1987.

Home, Henry. *Elements of Criticism*. 2 vols. 6th ed. Edinburgh, 1785.

Hume, David. *An Enquiry Concerning Human Understanding*. Edited by Eric Steinberg. Indianapolis and Cambridge: Hackett, 1993.

——. *Essays, Moral, Political, and Literary*. Oxford: Oxford University Press, 1971.

Hutcheson, Francis. *An Inquiry into the Original of our Ideas of Beauty and Virtue*. 4th ed. London, 1738.

Irwin, William (ed.). *The Death and Resurrection of the Author*. Westport, CT: Greenwood Press, 2002.

James, William. *Essays in Pragmatism*. Edited by Alburey Castell. New York: Hafner, 1951.

Kac, Mark. *Enigmas of Chance: An Autobiography*. New York: Harper and Row, 1985.

Kant, Immanuel. *Critique of Aesthetic Judgement*. Translated by James Creed Meredith. Oxford: Clarendon Press, 1911.

Kerman, Joseph. *The Beethoven Quartets*. New York: Alfred Knopf, 1967.

Kivy, Peter. "A Failure of Aesthetic Emotivism." *Philosophical Studies*, 38 (1980).

——. *Antithetical Arts: On the Ancient Quarrel Between Literature and Music*. Oxford: Clarendon Press, 2009.

——. "Fish's Consequences." *British Journal of Aesthetics*, 29 (1989).

——. "John Balguy and the Sense of Beauty: A Rational Realist in the Age of Sentiment." *Enlightenment and Dissent*, No. 23 (2004–7).

——. *Once-Told Tales: An Essay in Literary Aesthetics*. Chichester: Wiley-Blackwell, 2011.

——. *The Performance of Reading: An Essay in the Philosophy of Literature*. Oxford: Blackwell, 2006.

——. "Remarks on the Varieties of Prejudice in Hume's Essay on Taste." *The Journal of Scottish Philosophy*, 9 (2011).

——. *The Seventh Sense: Francis Hutcheson and Eighteenth-Century British Aesthetics*. 2nd ed. Oxford: Clarendon Press, 2003.

——. *Sounding Off: Eleven Essays in the Philosophy of Music*. Oxford: Oxford University Press, 2012.

——. *Speaking of Art*. The Hague: Martinus Nijhoff, 1973.

Landesman, Charles. *Leibniz's Mill: A Challenge to Materialism*. Notre Dame: University of Notre Dame Press, 2011.

Lewis, David. "Dispositional Theories of Value." *Proceedings of the Aristotelian Society*, Supplementary Volume, 63 (1989).

Melden, A. I. (ed.). *Ethical Theories: A Book of Readings*. New York: Prentice Hall, 1950.

Mill, John Stuart. *Utilitarianism*. Edited by Oskar Piest. New York: The Liberal Arts Press, 1957.

Olinder, Ragnar Francén. "Moral Relativism, Error Theory, and Ascriptions of Mistakes." *The Journal of Philosophy*, 110 (2013).

Olson, Jonas. "Projectivism and Error in Hume's Ethics," *Hume Studies*, 37 (2011).

Pippin, Robert B. *After the Beautiful: Hegel and the Philosophy of Pictorial Modernism*. Chicago and London: The University of Chicago Press, 2014.

Railton, Peter. "Moral Realism," *Philosophical Review*, 95 (1986).

Randel, Don Michael (ed.). *The Harvard Dictionary of Music*. Cambridge, MA, and London: The Belknap Press of Harvard University Press, 1978.

Redman, Alvin (ed.). *The Wit and Humor of Oscar Wilde*. New York: Dover Publications, 1959.

Reid, Thomas. *Lectures on the Fine Arts*. Edited by Peter Kivy. The Hague: Martinus Nijhoff, 1973.

——. *The Philosophical Works of Thomas Reid*. Edited by William Hamilton. 2 volumes. 8th ed. Edinburgh: James Thin, 1895.

Santayana, George. *The Sense of Beauty: Being an Outline of Aesthetic Theory*. New York: Random House, 1955.

Shafer-Landau, Russ. *Moral Realism: A Defense*. Oxford: Oxford University Press, 2005.

Sibley, Frank. "Aesthetic Concepts." *Philosophical Review*, 68 (1959).

Slote, Michael A. "The Rationality of Aesthetic Value Judgments." *The Journal of Philosophy*, 68 (1971).

Smith, Michael. "Dispositional Theories of Value." *Proceedings of the Aristotelian Society*, Supplementary Volume, 63 (1989).

Stevenson, Charles L. *Ethics and Language*. New Haven: Yale University Press, 1941.

——. *Facts and Values: Studies in Ethical Analysis*. New Haven and London: Yale University Press, 1963.

Streumer, Bart. "Can We Believe the Error Theory?" *The Journal of Philosophy*, 110 (2013).

Urmson, J. O. *The Emotive Theory of Ethics*. New York: Oxford University Press, 1969.

Index